D0501067

THE GREAT TRAINS

Luxury Rail Journeys of the World

THE GREAT TRAINS

Luxury Rail Journeys of the World

Timothy Wheaton

DORSET PRESS

This edition published by
Dorset Press,
a division of Marboro Books Corp,
by arrangement with Brompton Books Corporation.

Produced by Brompton Books Corporation
15 Sherwood Place
Greenwich, CT 06830

ISBN 0-88029-488-4

Printed in Hong Kong

Designed by Ruth DeJauregui
Captioned by Timothy Wheaton

Picture Credits

Geoffrey Freeman Allen 16 (top), 69
American-European Express 187, 188 (all), 189 (all)
American Graphic Systems Archives 4 (bottom), 29, 56-57 (top),77 (top), 108 (top), 124 (bottom), 158-159 (all), 165 (all), 166 (all), 170 (all), 174 (center, bottom), 175, 176 (all), 184 (all)
Amtrak 148 (all), 149 (all), 150 (top left, right)
Association of American Railroads 171
Rod Aszman 134, 146 (top left, right)
Australian News and Information Bureau 9
Baltimore & Ohio Railroad Museum 160 (top), 182 (all), 183
Bancroft Library, University of California at Berkeley 132 (top)
Brompton Picture Library 8-9 (bottom), 12-13, 28 (top), 40, 150 (bottom), 180-181
Don Buchholz 121
Canadian Pacific Corporate Archives 92-93 (all), 97 (all), 100-101 (all), 104-105, 114-115, 116 (left)
Cie Internationale des Wagons-Lits et du Tourisme 34, 60, 61
DeGolyer Library, Southern Methodist University 132 (bottom)
RE DeJauregui Collection 6, 24, 54, 66, 74, 90, 120, 156, 186
Arthur Dubin Collection 179 (all)
Paul Hansen 68 (center, bottom)
Nils Huxtable's Steamscenes 7, 12-13, 20-21, 25, 36-37, 44-45, 49, 50-51, 53, 55, 58-59, 62-63, 75, 79, 81 (top), 84 (top), 91, 98-99, 102-103, 107, 109, 110-111, 117, 118-119, 130-131, 134-135, 138 (top), 139, 147, 153 (bottom), 154-155, 158 (top), 159, 167, 172-173, 177, 192
Intourist 60-61
Intraflug 46 (top)
Timothy Jacobs Collection 64 (top left)
Japan National Tourist Office 67, 69 (bottom), 70, 70-71 (top), 72
Mrs V Johnstone/Battye Library 8
Mansell Collection 47 (all)
Milwaukee Road 185 (all)
National Railway Museum 27, 34-35
Peter Newark's Western Americana 95
Nostalgic Istanbul Orient Express 29 (bottom), 33 (bottom), 37, 41, 43 (bottom), 52 (center)
New York Central System Historical Society, Inc, Purinton Collection 178 (bottom), 181
Railways of Australia 8-9 (top), 10-11, 13, 18, 19, 22-23 (all)
ScanAm/STC 64 (top right)
Don Sims 186 (top)
South African Transport Services 2-3, 76 (all), 77 (bottom), 78 (all), 80 (all), 81 (bottom), 82-83, 84 (center, bottom), 85 (all), 86-87
Southern Pacific 1, 122-123 (all), 124 (top), 125 (top right), 126-127 (all), 128 (all), 129 (all), 133, 136-137, 138 9bottom), 140-141 (all), 142-143, 144 (all), 145, 153 (top), 157, 160 (bottom),161, 164-165, 168-169
Stan F Styles 94-95 (center, bottom), 96 (all)
Union Pacific 174 (top)
UPI/Bettman 178 (top)
Venice-Simplon Orient Express 26, 26-27, 30-31, 32 (all), 33 (top), 38-39 (all), 40-41, 42 (all), 43 (top), 48 (all), 52 (top, bottom)
VIA Rail 94-95 (top), 105 (all), 106 (all), 108 (bottom), 113 (all), 114-115, 116 (right)
Patty Warren's Antiques, Sacramento, California 4 (top), 5 (all),16 (top), 51, 56-57 (bottom), 88-89, 146 (bottom)
Westrail 14-15 (all), 17, 18-19
John Westwood 64-65, 78-79
© Bill Yenne 68 (top), 70-71 (bottom), 72-73, 151, 152 (all), 154-155, 162-163

Page 1: Mom buys the tickets while her little girl espies a kindred spirit, at a Union Pacific passenger station in 1939. _Pages 2–3:_ The luxurious _Blue Train_ of South Africa. _These pages, left to right below:_ A streamlined 4-6-2 locomotive like those that hauled the _Orient Express_ in the 1930s; an Astra-Dome observation lounge on a Southern Pacific special of the 1960s; the _Twentieth Century Limited_, in the 1950s; and Union Station in Chicago, a hub for many of America's great trains.

Contents

Australia's **Indian-Pacific** Transcontinental Express 6
The **Venice-Simplon** and the **Nostalgie Istanbul Orient Express** 24
The USSR's **Trans-Siberian Express** 54
Japan's **Shinkansen** 'Bullet Trains' 66
The **Blue Train** of South Africa 74
Canada's VIA Rail **Canadian** 90
The USA's Southern Pacific **Daylight** 120
A Tour of the USA on Great Trains of the 1950s 156
The USA's **American-European Express** 186
Index 190

Australia's Indian-Pacific Transcontinental Express

*The **Indian-Pacific** is named for the two oceans that it connects in its heroic 3960-km (2461 miles) journey across the Australian continent. The train mounts several steep gradients (one in 33 just outside of Sydney, for example), and traverses a vast, arid and virtually uninhabited wasteland that is called the Nullarbor Plain.*

This train's route, from Sydney to Perth via Adelaide, is the newest transcontinental route in the world, having been opened in 1969. This service was a major advance in Australian travel. Prior to this, trans-Australian travel required transfers to a number of trains, due to the varying track widths that the provinces used.

The Sydney to Perth route is built to standard gauge, or 1435 mm (four feet, eight inches) in width, and its central component is the original Trans-Australian Railway, which was built to standard gauge in 1917.

In itself, the Trans-Australian Railway has an interesting history. Near the turn of the century, most Australian provinces were interested in uniting as a single federation. Only Western Australia, isolated as it was

by the arid reaches of the Nullarbor Plain, hung back.

Western Australia was lured into agreeing to unification by a proposal to build the Trans-Australian Railway, which would run from Port Augusta—on Spencer Gulf in South Australia—to Kalgoorlie—1693 km (1052 miles) west in Western Australia. Plans were being made for this. The Commonwealth of Australia became a reality on 1 January 1901.

The flat, arid land of the west was so hostile that surveying parties had to be completely provisioned, as there was no chance of 'living off the land.' Temperatures in the Nullarbor Plain range from well below freezing in the winter to 50 degrees Celsius (122 degrees Fahrenheit) in the summer.

Finally, on 14 September 1912, work commenced. This involved wells that had to be sunk and reservoirs that had to be constructed to provide water for work parties. Despite the hazards of exposure and dehydration, track workers completed the line in four years, and it was open for traffic in 1917. That same year, the historic *Trans-Australian Express*, a symbol of national unity, was inaugurated on the line.

The completed Trans-Australian Railway was 1691 km (1051 miles) in length. There were no settlements extant along most of its route, and there was no possibility of making spur lines to existing railroads south of the line, as track gauges varied.

As train crews needed refreshment and steam locomotives needed fuel and water, station stops had to be built to provide for them. Three depots—Tarcoola, Cook and Rawlinna—were built at locations that divided the line into four roughly equal segments. In time, more little communities sprang up along the line to serve the needs of the railroad.

Even with this line, transcontinental travel in Australia was complex. If a first-class passenger wanted to go from Sydney, on the east coast, to Perth, on the west, the first leg of the trip would be achieved in the comfort of a New South Wales Railway drawing room suite aboard the *Melbourne Limited*, drawn by a sleek and fast 4-6-2 Pacific steam locomotive.

At the border of Victoria, a change of track gauge would necessitate boarding the Victorian Railways' blue and gold

Vintage photos. *Previous page:* The *Indian-Pacific* at Lithgow. *Above:* A Western Australian Government steam locomotive.

special, *Spirit of Progress*, with full air conditioning and an observation car. At Melbourne, another change of trains to Victorian Railways' *Overland* streamliner would be necessitated by the one-in-37 gradients of the Mount Lofty Range, east of Adelaide.

After the *Overland*'s powerful 4-8-4 Northern-type locomotive pulled into Adelaide, South Australian Railways' *East-West Express* would get the passenger to Port Pirie, on Spencer Gulf. At Port Pirie, a change of trains was made to Commonwealth Railways' *Trans-Australian Express*. Here, too, a change of track gauge was made, from the 1600 mm (five feet, three inches) gauge of South Australian Railways, to the 1435 mm gauge (four feet, eight inches) of the nationalized Trans-Australian Railway.

The *Trans-Australian Express* was quite luxurious for its time, with on-board showers in its first-class sleeper cars as of 1918, and diner and lounge cars with air conditioning as of 1936. The lounge also featured a piano, on which passengers could while away the hours.

This train was powered by inglamorous 4-6-0s that were dwarfed by tenders big enough to compensate for the dearth of locomotive supplies along the way. After two days of travel through the Nullarbor Plain and environs, the *Trans-Australian Express* pulled into Kalgoorlie, mid-way across Western Australia. Here, a change of trains and track gauge was made. The passenger boarded the Western Australian Government Railways' *Westland* express train, riding on that railway's 1067 mm gauge (three feet, six inches) tracks.

Though the track was narrow, the *Westland*'s stainless steel sleeper cars were built to a roomy width of nine feet and were equipped with showers. This last leg of the trip took 15 hours, and traversed the Darling Mountains from Kalgoorlie to Perth, on the west coast of Australia. Altogether, such a transcontinental journey was 4475 km (2781 miles) in length.

The transcontinental through service that made the *Indian-Pacific* a reality was inspired by the building of a

The *Trans-Continental*. *Above left:* Construction of the line. *At left:* A vintage parlor car. *Above:* The straight stretch.

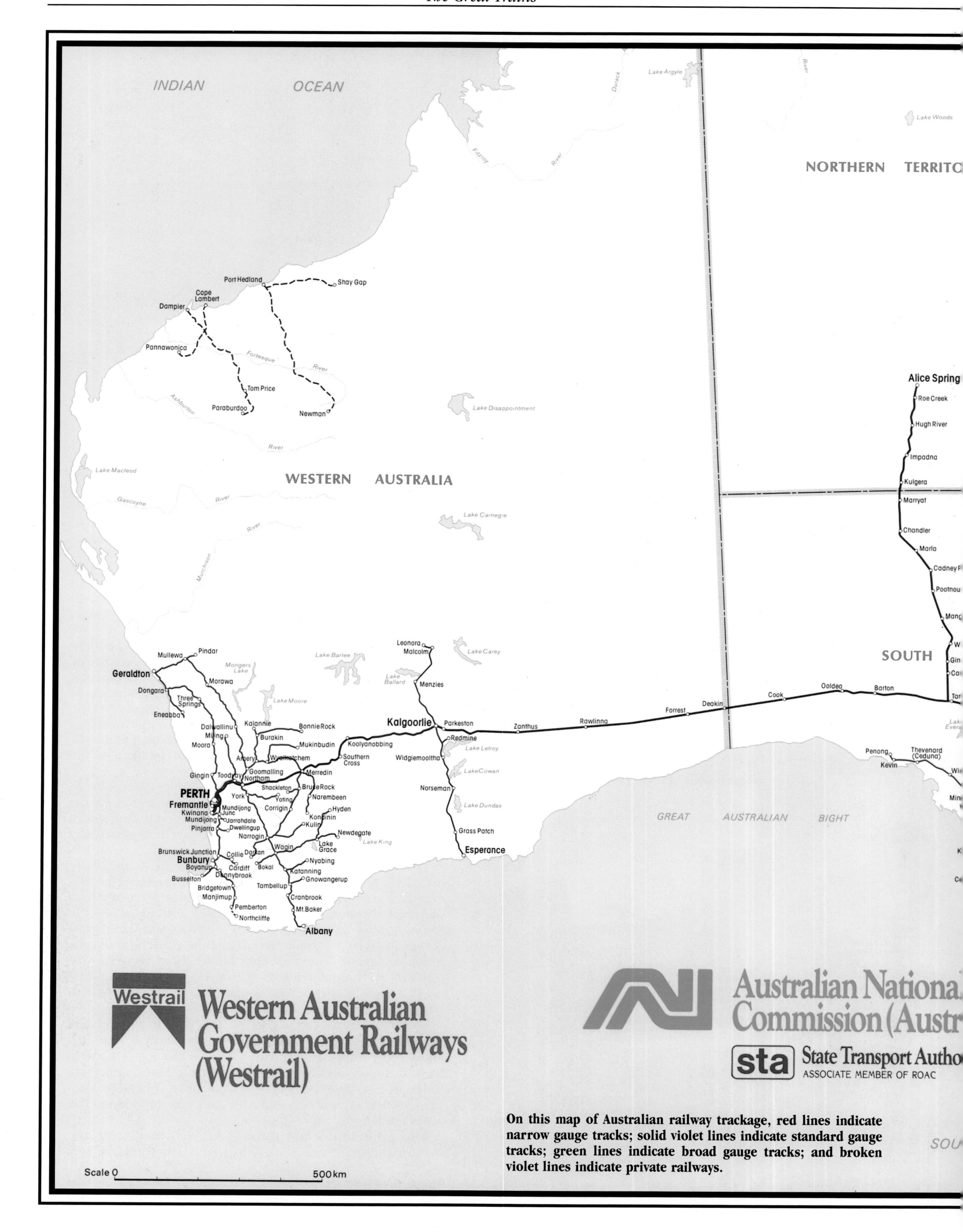

On this map of Australian railway trackage, red lines indicate narrow gauge tracks; solid violet lines indicate standard gauge tracks; green lines indicate broad gauge tracks; and broken violet lines indicate private railways.

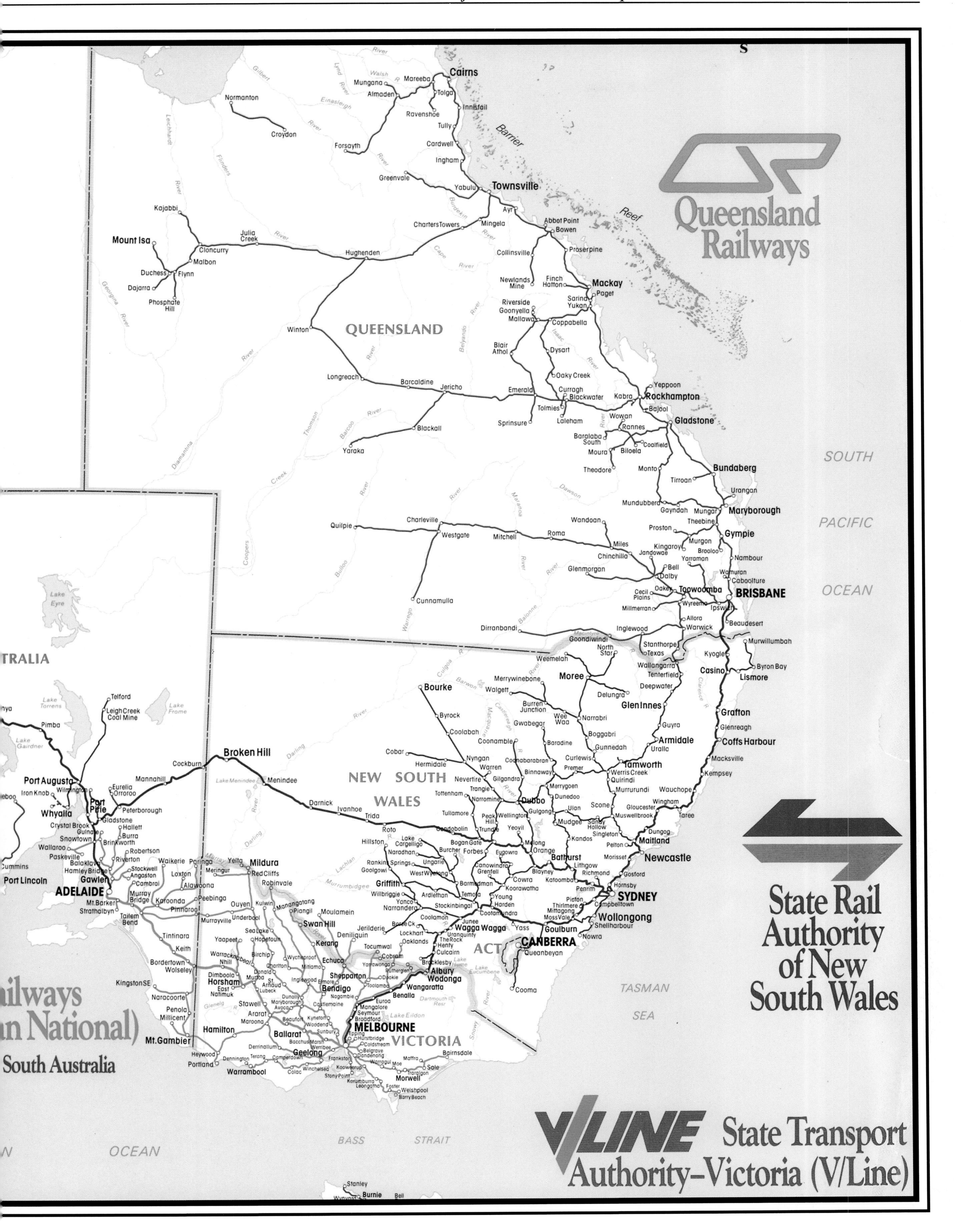
Queensland Railways
State Rail Authority of New South Wales
V/LINE State Transport Authority–Victoria (V/Line)
ailways
an National)
South Australia
QUEENSLAND
NEW SOUTH WALES
VICTORIA
ACT
TRALIA
SOUTH PACIFIC OCEAN
TASMAN SEA
OCEAN
BASS STRAIT
Barrier Reef
Cairns
Mareeba
Mungana
Almaden
Tolga
Innisfail
Ravenshoe
Tully
Cardwell
Ingham
Normanton
Croydon
Forsayth
Greenvale
Yabulu
Townsville
Ayr
Abbot Point
Bowen
Kajabbi
Mount Isa
Julia Creek
Cloncurry
Malbon
Duchess
Flynn
Dajarra
Phosphate Hill
Hughenden
Charters Towers
Mingela
Collinsville
Proserpine
Newlands Mine
Finch Hatton
Mackay
Paget
Sarina
Yukan
Riverside
Goonyella
Mallawa
Coppabella
Winton
Blair Athol
Dysart
Oaky Creek
Longreach
Barcaldine
Jericho
Emerald
Curragh
Blackwater
Kabra
Yeppoon
Rockhampton
Bajool
Tolmies
Laleham
Sprinsure
Blackall
Yaraka
Gladstone
Wowan
Rannes
Baralaba South
Moura
Biloela
Coalfield
Theodore
Monto
Bundaberg
Tirroan
Urangan
Mundubbera
Gayndah
Mungar
Maryborough
Theebine
Gympie
Wandoan
Charleville
Quilpie
Westgate
Mitchell
Roma
Miles
Chinchilla
Proston
Kingaroy
Murgon
Jandowae
Brooloo
Yarraman
Nambour
Glenmorgan
Bell
Dalby
Caboolture
Oakey
Toowoomba
BRISBANE
Cecil Plains
Millmerran
Wyreema
Ipswich
Cunnamulla
Allora
Warwick
Beaudesert
Dirranbandi
Inglewood
Goondiwindi
North Star
Stanthorpe
Texas
Murwillumbah
Weemelah
Kyogle
Byron Bay
Wallangarra
Tenterfield
Casino
Lismore
Moree
Merrywinebone
Walgett
Bourke
Deepwater
Delungra
Glen Innes
Burren Junction
Wee Waa
Narrabri
Grafton
Glenreagh
Byrock
Gwabegar
Guyra
Coolabah
Boggabri
Armidale
Coffs Harbour
Coonamble
Baradine
Gunnedah
Uralla
Cobar
Hermidale
Nyngan
Coonabarabran
Curlewis
Tamworth
Macksville
Warren
Binnaway
Premer
Werris Creek
Quirindi
Kempsey
Nevertire
Gilgandra
Trangie
Merrygoen
Murrurundi
Wauchope
Tottenham
Narromine
Dubbo
Dunedoo
Wingham
Tullamore
Peak Hill
Wellington
Gulgong
Ulan
Scone
Gloucester
Muswellbrook
Taree
Condobolin
Trundle
Yeoval
Mudgee
Sandy Hollow
Singleton
Dungog
Maitland
Kandos
Bogan Gate
Molong
Orange
Pelton
Newcastle
Lake Cargelligo
Naradhan
Burcher
Forbes
Eugowra
Bathurst
Morisset
Hillston
Rankins Springs
Ungarie
Lithgow
Goolgowi
West Wyalong
Canowindra
Grenfell
Blayney
Richmond
Gosford
Katoomba
Hornsby
Griffith
Barmedman
Cowra
Koorawatha
Penrith
SYDNEY
Willbriggie
Yanco
Ardlethan
Temora
Young
Harden
Picton
Thirlmere
Mittagong
Campbelltown
Narrandera
Stockinbingal
Cootamundra
Moss Vale
Wollongong
Shellharbour
Coolamon
Junee
Wagga Wagga
Yass
Goulburn
Nowra
CANBERRA
Queanbeyan
Jerilderie
Berrigan
Lockhart
The Rock
Uranquinty
Henty
Culcairn
Oaklands
Tocumwal
Cooma
Broken Hill
Menindee
Cockburn
Mannahill
Darnick
Ivanhoe
Trida
Roto
Telford
Leigh Creek Coal Mine
Lake Torrens
Lake Frome
Lake Eyre
Lake Gairdner
Pimba
Port Augusta
Wilmington
Eurelia
Orroroo
Iron Knob
Whyalla
Port Pirie
Peterborough
Crystal Brook
Gladstone
Hallett
Gulnare
Burra
Snowtown
Brinkworth
Wallaroo
Robertson
Paskeville
Riverton
Balaklava
Hamley Bridge
Stockwell
Angaston
Waikerie
Paringa
Yelta
Mildura
Red Cliffs
Meringur
Loxton
Cummins
Port Lincoln
Gawler
Cambrai
ADELAIDE
Alawoona
Robinvale
Murray Bridge
Karoonda
Mt. Barker
Strathalbyn
Peebinga
Pinnaroo
Ouyen
Kulwin
Manangatang
Piangil
Moulamein
Tailem Bend
Murrayville
Underbool
Swan Hill
Deniliquin
Tintinara
Sea Lake
Hopetoun
Yaapeet
Kerang
Keith
Bordertown
Wolseley
Nhill
Birchip
Echuca
Kingston SE
Dimboola
Horsham
Natimuk
Donald
Charlton
St Arnaud
Shepparton
Dookie
Bendigo
Benalla
Wangaratta
Albury
Wodonga
Naracoorte
Penola
Millicent
Stawell
Ararat
Maroona
Castlemaine
Mangalore
Seymour
Broadford
MELBOURNE
Hamilton
Ballarat
Mt. Gambier
Heywood
Portland
Dennington
Terang
Camperdown
Warrnambool
Geelong
Colac
Frankston
Bairnsdale
Maffra
Sale
Traralgon
Morwell
Stony Point
Korumburra
Leongatha
Welshpool
Barry Beach
Stanley
Wynyard
Burnie
Bell

much-needed standard-gauge ore line, stretching from Koolyanobbing, 37 miles west of Kalgoorlie, to the Australian Iron & Steel Company mills at Kwinana, just south of Perth. This line effectively displaced the Western Australian Government Railways narrow-gauge track for through travel from South Australia to the west coast, and inspired an effort to create a single, standard gauge line across the entire country.

South Australia agreed to re-gauge its 216-mile stretch of track from Port Pirie to Cockburn (on the New South Wales border), reducing the trackwidth from 1600 mm (five feet, three inches) to standard gauge, in order to match the Trans-Australian Railway tracks coming from the west to Port Pirie.

It should be said that the new standard-gauge tracks passed through Coonamia, just west of Port Pirie. Hence, Port Pirie was left stranded on the old narrow gauge track. The standard gauge tracks were a match for the New South Wales standard gauge tracks coming into Cockburn from the east. These tracks from the east ran to Sydney, and made for a straighter route to the east coast than the old roundabout trackage southward through Victoria, via Melbourne.

New South Wales upgraded this trackage from Sydney to Cockburn, to ensure smooth running all along the way. Therefore, a single, standard-gauge ran from coast to coast. It was completed in 1969, and is 3960 km (2461 miles) long.

Australia's new flagship train, the *Indian-Pacific*, was created especially for the route. It was seen as symbolic and fitting that the nation's premier train should connect its two oceans in fact as well as name. *Indian-Pacific* service was inaugurated in 1970. It is a very luxurious train, with roomy, two-berth compartments in the first-class cars. These compartments are called 'twinettes,' and are each equipped with a wardrobe closet, a private shower and toilet facilities.

It is possible to expand a twinette for family travel by means of a door connecting one twinette with another, adjoining twinette. Single, first-class rooms are also available, but these have only a private toilet. Both first-class and economy-class passengers have free access to the shower facilities at the ends of the sleeping cars, as well.

Also, at least one *Indian-Pacific* schedule allows the economy-class passenger twinette service. Every compartment has ice water for drinking on tap, as well as hot and

At left: **An exhibition restoration of the *Melbourne Limited*.**
Above: **Electric power hauls the *Indian-Pacific* to Lithgow.**

cold wash water; plus a built-in radio with a choice of programs, and power-operated venetian blinds that are sandwiched between the dual glass panes of the windows. More economically-minded passengers can choose to travel coach class, wherein sleeping facilities are reclining aircraft-style seats. Shower and changing facilities are availed to these passengers as well.

A cafeteria/club car provides drinks and light refreshments for all passengers. First class lounge cars are equipped with pianos or electric organs, for musically talented passengers to enjoy; and also have a selection of videotape programs and recorded music that can be played; as well as a full range of refreshing beverages.

Some *Indian-Pacific* schedules have car-carrier service as well, and will allow passengers to bring their vehicles along with them for easy travel at their destination.

Early morning room service provides complimentary tea and biscuits, and afternoon tea is served the same, but sleeping berth passengers have most of their on-board meals in the diner. Breakfast offerings include eggs any style, bacon, sausage, sirloin minute steak and grilled lamb chops. In combination with any of these courses are biscuits, scones or toast and tea, fruit juice or coffee.

The average *Indian-Pacific* lunch menu presents soup as an opener, then offers a tantalizing choice of Chicken Mornay or fish fillet, followed by a selection of side dishes, including eggs and asparagus; roast turkey and ham; or a plate of cold meats. This is followed by desserts ranging from baked lemon rice pudding to a fruit sundae, and the meal is topped off by cheese and biscuits.

A representative dinner aboard the *Indian-Pacific* begins with fruit salad or soup, and proceeds to a baked fillet of fish with anchovy sauce. The next course may well be a choice of grilled steak with sauce Bearnaise, or roast turkey and

***Above:* Dinner aboard the *Indian-Pacific*. *Above opposite:* Relaxing in the lounge. *At right:* The *Indian-Pacific*.**

ham, or roast leg of pork. Dessert may be a Dutch apple tart with cream, an apricot trifle or a Neapolitan ice. This meal is customarily concluded with a savory cheese dish.

The *Indian-Pacific* does not fly along, but rather lulls the passenger with a gentle approach to speed, averaging 80 kph (50 mph) for the entire journey, although there are stretches—notably on the western plains—when it does attain 113 kph (70 mph).

On the first day of an east-west *Indian-Pacific* journey, passengers gather at the terminal in Sydney, one of Australia's most important cities, and home of the futuristic, world-renowned Sydney Opera House; popular Luna Park amusement fair; Bondi Beach, a center for that favorite Australian activity, sun bathing; and the impressive steel arch span of Sydney Harbor Bridge—like the Sydney Opera House, a national landmark.

The train departs the terminal at 13:30, and is soon climbing toward the 1067-meter (3503 feet) summit of the Blue Mountains, just west of Sydney. In colder weather, passengers may well see snow on the upper slopes of these mountains. All the way from Sydney and up the steep eastern inclines of these rugged mountains, the train is pulled by a powerful electric locomotive.

At Lithgow, which marks the apex of the climb, the electric engine is uncoupled from the train, and is replaced by a diesel locomotive. In fact, the gradients in the Blue Mountains are so steep that the train is often hauled up in sections, and is then 'reassembled' at Lithgow. Once out of the Blue Mountains, the *Indian-Pacific* commences its nighttime trek across the monotonous western New South Wales scrubland plain.

At 8:10 of the second day, the train arrives at Broken Hill, where the world's richest deposit of silver and lead has been mined continuously since the late 1860s. With 20 minutes to stretch their legs, passengers have the chance to inspect the town's attractive Victorian architecture.

Here, the *Indian-Pacific* replenishes its train water, and

trades its New South Wales diesel locomotive for a South Australian one, as the provinces provide the motive power for this service. The train departs Broken Hill at 8:30, crossing the desolate speargrass-covered flatland of eastern South Australia. This might be a good time to relax in the first-class lounge, or read a book, though some excitement might be generated by the sudden occurrence of a regional dust storm, raging just beyond the air conditioned and purified atmosphere of the train.

The *Indian-Pacific* pulls into Adelaide at 16:00. Adelaide's many attractions include the South Australian Museum, in the North Terrace neighborhood; fascinating architecture; the beach on St Vincent's Gulf; and surrounding environs that host a yearly series of events that include the German Festival and the highly popular Vintner's Festival.

Since passengers won't have sufficient time to partake of these delights on their *Indian-Pacific* trip, they may be inspiration for prolonged stays in Australia, which are facilitated by such as the excellent *Overland* overnight train service from Melbourne to Adelaide, which provides car carrier service.

Another excellent Adelaide-area transport is *The Ghan*, an overnight train that runs between Adelaide and Alice Springs, a favorite mountain playground for South Australians. Also departing from Adelaide is the *Trans-Australian*, which runs to Perth along the same route as the *Indian-Pacific*. The *Overland*, *The Ghan* and the *Trans-Australian* provide their passengers much the same services as does the *Indian-Pacific*.

Above: **A view of a lounge car aboard the *Trans-Australian Express* earlier in this century. *At right:* A Blue Mountains vista. *Opposite:* A passenger diesel in Western Australia.**

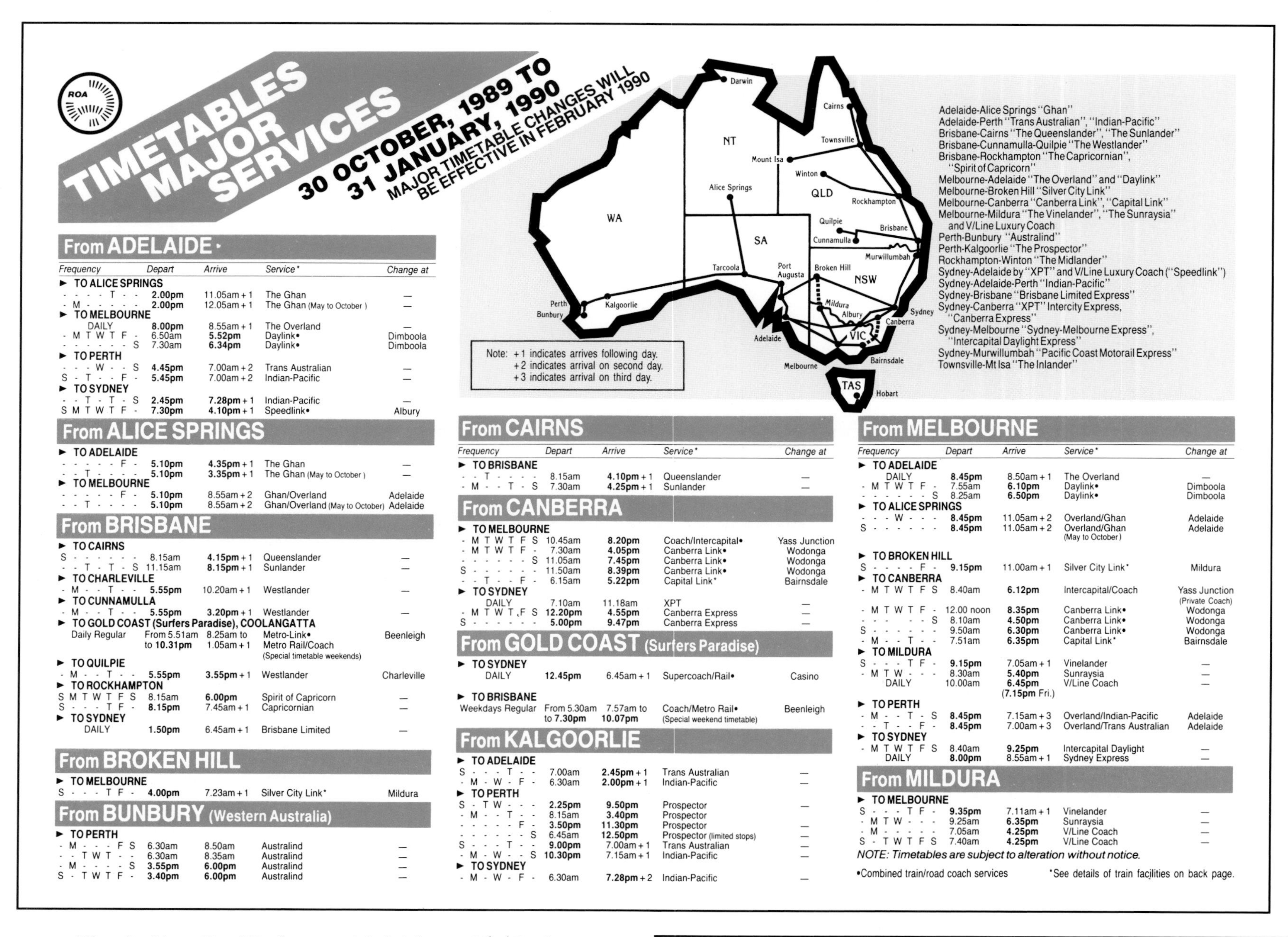

ROA

TIMETABLES MAJOR SERVICES

30 OCTOBER, 1989 TO 31 JANUARY, 1990

MAJOR TIMETABLE CHANGES WILL BE EFFECTIVE IN FEBRUARY 1990

Adelaide-Alice Springs "Ghan"
Adelaide-Perth "Trans Australian", "Indian-Pacific"
Brisbane-Cairns "The Queenslander", "The Sunlander"
Brisbane-Cunnamulla-Quilpie "The Westlander"
Brisbane-Rockhampton "The Capricornian", "Spirit of Capricorn"
Melbourne-Adelaide "The Overland" and "Daylink"
Melbourne-Broken Hill "Silver City Link"
Melbourne-Canberra "Canberra Link", "Capital Link"
Melbourne-Mildura "The Vinelander", "The Sunraysia" and V/Line Luxury Coach
Perth-Bunbury "Australind"
Perth-Kalgoorlie "The Prospector"
Rockhampton-Winton "The Midlander"
Sydney-Adelaide by "XPT" and V/Line Luxury Coach ("Speedlink")
Sydney-Adelaide-Perth "Indian-Pacific"
Sydney-Brisbane "Brisbane Limited Express"
Sydney-Canberra "XPT" Intercity Express, "Canberra Express"
Sydney-Melbourne "Sydney-Melbourne Express", "Intercapital Daylight Express"
Sydney-Murwillumbah "Pacific Coast Motorail Express"
Townsville-Mt Isa "The Inlander"

Note: +1 indicates arrives following day.
+2 indicates arrival on second day.
+3 indicates arrival on third day.

From ADELAIDE

Frequency	Depart	Arrive	Service*	Change at
► TO ALICE SPRINGS				
- - - - T - -	**2.00pm**	11.05am + 1	The Ghan	—
- M - - - - -	**2.00pm**	12.05am + 1	The Ghan (May to October)	—
► TO MELBOURNE				
DAILY	**8.00pm**	8.55am + 1	The Overland	—
- M T W T F -	6.50am	**5.52pm**	Daylink•	Dimboola
- - - - - - S	7.30am	**6.34pm**	Daylink•	Dimboola
► TO PERTH				
- - - W - - S	**4.45pm**	7.00am + 2	Trans Australian	—
S - T - - F -	**5.45pm**	7.00am + 2	Indian-Pacific	—
► TO SYDNEY				
- - T - T - S	**2.45pm**	**7.28pm** + 1	Indian-Pacific	—
S M T W T F -	**7.30pm**	**4.10pm** + 1	Speedlink•	Albury

From ALICE SPRINGS

Frequency	Depart	Arrive	Service*	Change at
► TO ADELAIDE				
- - - - - F -	**5.10pm**	**4.35pm** + 1	The Ghan	—
- - T - - - -	**5.10pm**	**3.35pm** + 1	The Ghan (May to October)	—
► TO MELBOURNE				
- - - - - F -	**5.10pm**	8.55am + 2	Ghan/Overland	Adelaide
- - T - - - -	**5.10pm**	8.55am + 2	Ghan/Overland (May to October)	Adelaide

From BRISBANE

Frequency	Depart	Arrive	Service*	Change at
► TO CAIRNS				
S - - - - - -	8.15am	**4.15pm** + 1	Queenslander	—
- - T - T - S	11.15am	**8.15pm** + 1	Sunlander	—
► TO CHARLEVILLE				
- M - - T - -	**5.55pm**	10.20am + 1	Westlander	—
► TO CUNNAMULLA				
- M - - T - -	**5.55pm**	**3.20pm** + 1	Westlander	—
► TO GOLD COAST (Surfers Paradise), COOLANGATTA				
Daily Regular	From 5.51am to **10.31pm**	8.25am to 1.05am + 1	Metro-Link• Metro Rail/Coach (Special timetable weekends)	Beenleigh
► TO QUILPIE				
- M - - T - -	**5.55pm**	**3.55pm** + 1	Westlander	Charleville
► TO ROCKHAMPTON				
S M T W T F S	8.15am	**6.00pm**	Spirit of Capricorn	—
S - - - T F -	**8.15pm**	7.45am + 1	Capricornian	—
► TO SYDNEY				
DAILY	**1.50pm**	6.45am + 1	Brisbane Limited	—

From BROKEN HILL

Frequency	Depart	Arrive	Service*	Change at
► TO MELBOURNE				
S - - - T F -	**4.00pm**	7.23am + 1	Silver City Link*	Mildura

From BUNBURY (Western Australia)

Frequency	Depart	Arrive	Service*	Change at
► TO PERTH				
- M - - - F S	6.30am	8.50am	Australind	—
- - T W T - -	6.30am	8.35am	Australind	—
- M - - - - S	**3.55pm**	**6.00pm**	Australind	—
S - T W T F -	**3.40pm**	**6.00pm**	Australind	—

From CAIRNS

Frequency	Depart	Arrive	Service*	Change at
► TO BRISBANE				
- - T - - - -	8.15am	**4.10pm** + 1	Queenslander	—
- M - - T - S	7.30am	**4.25pm** + 1	Sunlander	—

From CANBERRA

Frequency	Depart	Arrive	Service*	Change at
► TO MELBOURNE				
- M T W T F S	10.45am	**8.20pm**	Coach/Intercapital•	Yass Junction
- M T W T F -	7.30am	**4.05pm**	Canberra Link•	Wodonga
- - - - - - S	11.05am	**7.45pm**	Canberra Link•	Wodonga
S - - - - - -	11.50am	**8.39pm**	Canberra Link•	Wodonga
- - T - - F -	6.15am	**5.22pm**	Capital Link*	Bairnsdale
► TO SYDNEY				
DAILY	7.10am	11.18am	XPT	—
- M T W T F S	**12.20pm**	**4.55pm**	Canberra Express	—
S - - - - - -	**5.00pm**	**9.47pm**	Canberra Express	—

From GOLD COAST (Surfers Paradise)

Frequency	Depart	Arrive	Service*	Change at
► TO SYDNEY				
DAILY	**12.45pm**	6.45am + 1	Supercoach/Rail•	Casino
► TO BRISBANE				
Weekdays Regular	From 5.30am to **7.30pm**	7.57am to **10.07pm**	Coach/Metro Rail• (Special weekend timetable)	Beenleigh

From KALGOORLIE

Frequency	Depart	Arrive	Service*	Change at
► TO ADELAIDE				
S - - - T - -	7.00am	**2.45pm** + 1	Trans Australian	—
- M - W - F -	6.30am	**2.00pm** + 1	Indian-Pacific	—
► TO PERTH				
S - T W - - -	**2.25pm**	**9.50pm**	Prospector	—
- M - - T - -	8.15am	**3.40pm**	Prospector	—
- - - - - F -	**3.50pm**	**11.30pm**	Prospector	—
- - - - - - S	6.45am	**12.50pm**	Prospector (limited stops)	—
S - - - T - -	**9.00pm**	7.00am + 1	Trans Australian	—
- M - W - - S	**10.30pm**	7.15am + 1	Indian-Pacific	—
► TO SYDNEY				
- M - W - F -	6.30am	**7.28pm** + 2	Indian-Pacific	—

From MELBOURNE

Frequency	Depart	Arrive	Service*	Change at
► TO ADELAIDE				
DAILY	**8.45pm**	8.50am + 1	The Overland	—
- M T W T F -	7.55am	**6.10pm**	Daylink•	Dimboola
- - - - - - S	8.25am	**6.50pm**	Daylink•	Dimboola
► TO ALICE SPRINGS				
- - - W - - -	**8.45pm**	11.05am + 2	Overland/Ghan	Adelaide
S - - - - - -	**8.45pm**	11.05am + 2	Overland/Ghan (May to October)	Adelaide
► TO BROKEN HILL				
S - - - - F -	**9.15pm**	11.00am + 1	Silver City Link*	Mildura
► TO CANBERRA				
- M T W T F S	8.40am	**6.12pm**	Intercapital/Coach	Yass Junction (Private Coach)
- M T W T F -	12.00 noon	**8.35pm**	Canberra Link•	Wodonga
- - - - - - S	8.10am	**4.50pm**	Canberra Link•	Wodonga
S - - - - - -	9.50am	**6.30pm**	Canberra Link•	Wodonga
- M - - T - -	7.51am	**6.35pm**	Capital Link*	Bairnsdale
► TO MILDURA				
S - - - T F -	**9.15pm**	7.05am + 1	Vinelander	—
- M T W - - -	8.30am	**5.40pm**	Sunraysia	—
DAILY	10.00am	**6.45pm** (**7.15pm** Fri.)	V/Line Coach	—
► TO PERTH				
- M - - T - S	**8.45pm**	7.15am + 3	Overland/Indian-Pacific	Adelaide
- - T - - F -	**8.45pm**	7.00am + 3	Overland/Trans Australian	Adelaide
► TO SYDNEY				
- M T W T F S	8.40am	**9.25pm**	Intercapital Daylight	—
DAILY	**8.00pm**	8.55am + 1	Sydney Express	—

From MILDURA

Frequency	Depart	Arrive	Service*	Change at
► TO MELBOURNE				
S - - - T F -	**9.35pm**	7.11am + 1	Vinelander	—
- M T W - - -	9.25am	**6.35pm**	Sunraysia	—
- M - - - - -	7.05am	**4.25pm**	V/Line Coach	—
S - T W T F S	7.40am	**4.25pm**	V/Line Coach	—

NOTE: Timetables are subject to alteration without notice.

•Combined train/road coach services

*See details of train facilities on back page.

The *Indian-Pacific* leaves Adelaide at 16:45, three-quarters of an hour after its arrival. The train doubles back along its tracks for part of the evening journey to Coonamia, which is a brief stop at 19:40, and is the departure point for those wishing to take the old narrow-gauge railway to Port Pirie.

The route to Kalgoorlie features the vast and almost featureless Nullarbor Plain. Just past Ooldea, approximately 700 km (435 miles) westward of Coonamia, the world's longest straight stretch of track begins. The straightness and flatness of this 478-km (197-mile) track segment adds a feeling of suspension in a void to this portion of the passage through the sun-burnt, treeless flatland of the plain. The few vertical objects encountered on the surrounding flatness loom up over the horizon from the top down, as do objects seen from afar at sea: the horizon follows the actual curvature of the Earth.

However, the occasional appearance of an emu, dingo, kangaroo or camel may break the monotony that envelopes the train. This line section also allows some of the highest speeds on the *Indian-Pacific* run, thanks to ballast upgrades effected since 1970. It provides an excellent excuse to retreat to the lounge car for a film, a game of bridge, or some refreshment.

Nearly a whole day after leaving Coonamia, the train pulls into Kalgoorlie at 19:30. Kalgoorlie is the gold capital of Australia, and is full of historical attractions reminding visitors of the Australian Gold Rush. This town's importance is evidenced by the prestige of *The Prospector*, one of Australia's fastest trains, with *Indian-Pacific*-level amenities, that

***At right:* The *Indian-Pacific* at East Perth Rail Terminal, just previous to its evening return run to Sydney. This train is one of the most luxurious rail services on Earth.**

From MT ISA

Frequency	Depart	Arrive	Service*	Change at
► **TO TOWNSVILLE**				
- M - - - F -	**3.00pm**	7.45am + 1	Inlander	—

From MURWILLUMBAH (GOLD COAST)

Frequency	Depart	Arrive	Service*	Change at
► **TO SYDNEY**				
DAILY	**4.00pm**	9.03am + 1	Pacific Coast	—
DAILY	**1.56pm**	6.45am + 1	Supercoach/Rail•	Casino

From PERTH

Frequency	Depart	Arrive	Service*	Change at
► **TO ADELAIDE**				
- - - W - - S	**9.00pm**	**2.45pm** + 2	Trans Australian	—
S - T - T - -	**9.00pm**	**2.00pm** + 2	Indian-Pacific	—
► **TO BUNBURY**				
- M - - - - S	10.00am	12.00 noon	Australind	—
- - T W T F -	10.00am	**12.20pm**	Australind	—
S M - - - F S	**7.00pm**	**9.20pm**	Australind	—
- - T W T - -	**7.00pm**	**9.00pm**	Australind	—
► **TO KALGOORLIE**				
S M - W - - -	**3.00pm**	**10.40pm**	Prospector	—
- - T - T - -	9.00am	**4.35pm**	Prospector	—
- - - - - F -	**3.35pm**	**9.35pm**	Prospector (non-stop)	—
- - - - - F -	**4.20pm**	12.20am + 1	Prospector	—
► **TO MELBOURNE**				
S - T - T - -	**9.00pm**	8.55am + 3	Indian-Pacific/Overland	Adelaide
- - - W - - S	**9.00pm**	8.55am + 3	Trans Australian/Overland	Adelaide
► **TO SYDNEY**				
S - T - T - -	**9.00pm**	**7.28pm** + 3	Indian-Pacific	—

From ROCKHAMPTON

Frequency	Depart	Arrive	Service*	Change at
► **TO BRISBANE**				
S M T W T F S	8.15am	**6.00pm**	Spirit of Capricorn	—
S - - - T F -	**7.20pm**	6.40am + 1	Capricornian	—
- - - W - - -	5.40am	**4.10pm**	Queenslander	—
S - T - - F -	5.45am	**4.25pm**	Sunlander	—
► **TO CAIRNS**				
S - - - - - -	**6.50pm**	**4.15pm** + 1	Queenslander	—
- - T - T - S	**10.20pm**	**8.15pm** + 1	Sunlander	—
► **TO WINTON**				
- - T - - F -	**6.45pm**	**12.20pm** + 1	Midlander	—

From SYDNEY

Frequency	Depart	Arrive	Service*	Change at
► **TO ADELAIDE**				
- M - - T - S	**1.30pm**	**5.00pm** + 1	Indian-Pacific	—
- M T W T F S	**12.15pm**	7.40am + 1	Speedlink•	Albury
► **TO BRISBANE**				
DAILY	**6.05pm**	10.35am + 1	Brisbane Limited	—
► **TO CANBERRA**				
DAILY	7.30am	12.00 noon	Canberra Express	—
DAILY	**6.40pm**	**10.50pm**	XPT	—
► **TO GOLD COAST (Surfers Paradise)**				
DAILY	**6.05pm**	11.12am + 1	Rail/Supercoach•	Casino
► **TO MELBOURNE**				
DAILY	**8.00pm**	9.00am + 1	Melbourne Express	—
- M T W T F S	7.45am	**8.20pm**	Intercapital Daylight	—
► **TO MURWILLUMBAH (for the Gold Coast)**				
DAILY	**6.25pm**	11.10am + 1	Pacific Coast	—
DAILY	**6.05pm**	10.06am + 1	Rail/Supercoach•	Casino
► **TO PERTH**				
- M - - T - S	**1.30pm**	7.15am + 3	Indian-Pacific	—

NOTE: Timetables are subject to alteration without notice.

•Combined train/road coach services

*Details of train facilities.

FEATURES OF MAJOR SERVICES

	DELUXE CABIN	FIRST CLASS SLEEPERS	ECONOMY SLEEPERS	FIRST CLASS SITTING	COACH CAR SITTING	ECONOMY SITTING	LOUNGE/ CLUB CAR	DINING CAR	BUFFET CAR	MOTORAIL
Australind				Yes					Yes	
Brisbane Limited Express		Yes		Yes		Yes		Yes	Yes	Yes
Canberra XPT				Yes		Yes			Yes	
Canberra Express				Yes		Yes			Yes	
Canberra Link & Capital Link				Yes†		Yes			Coach stops†	
The Capricornian		Yes	Yes			Yes	Yes			
Daylink				Yes†		Yes			Coach stops†	
The Ghan	Yes	Yes			Yes		Yes	Yes	Yes	Yes
Indian-Pacific	Yes	Yes	Yes		Two Services only		Yes	Yes	Yes	Yes ★
The Inlander		Yes	Yes						Yes	
Intercapital Daylight Express				Yes		Yes			Yes	Yes
Melbourne Express	Yes	Yes		Yes		Yes	Yes	Yes	Yes	Yes
Metro-Link (Brisbane Metro Rail & Coach)						Yes				
The Midlander		Yes	Yes			Yes			Yes	
The Overland		Yes		Yes		Yes	Yes		Yes	Yes
Pacific Coast MotoRail Express		Yes		Yes		Yes		Yes	Yes	Yes
The Prospector				Yes				Meal provided		
The Queenslander		Yes				Yes	Yes	Yes		Yes
Silver City Link				Yes†		Yes			Coach stops†	
Speedlink				Yes		Yes			Coach stops†	
Spirit of Capricorn						Yes			Meal provided	
Supercoach/Rail						Yes			Coach stops†	
The Sunlander		Yes	Yes			Yes	Yes	Yes		
The Sunraysia				Yes		Yes			Yes	Yes
Sydney Express	Yes	Yes		Yes		Yes	Yes	Yes	Yes	Yes
Trans Australian		Yes	Yes		Yes		Yes	Yes	Yes	Yes
V/Line Road Coach						Yes			Coach stops	
The Vinelander		Yes		Yes		Yes			Yes	Yes
The Westlander		Yes	Yes			Yes			Yes	
XPT (Express Passenger Train)				Yes		Yes			Yes	

•Combined train/road coach services

†Yes — Trains only

★ Same train MotoRail services are available between Sydney-Adelaide, Adelaide-Perth and westbound Sydney-Perth. Eastbound MotoRail services between Perth-Sydney require an additional day in transit.

From TOWNSVILLE

Frequency	Depart	Arrive	Service*	Change at
► **TO MT ISA**				
S - - W - - -	**6.00pm**	11.55am + 1	Inlander	—

From SOUTH WEST QUEENSLAND

Frequency	Depart	Arrive	Service*	Change at
► **QUILPIE, CUNNAMULLA TO CHARLEVILLE AND BRISBANE**				
- - T - - F -	**5.25pm** (Quilpie)	**3.15pm** + 1	Westlander/ A/C Connection	Charleville
- - T - - F -	**5.55pm** (Cunnamulla)	**3.15pm** + 1	Westlander	—

From WINTON

Frequency	Depart	Arrive	Service*	Change at
► **TO ROCKHAMPTON**				
- - - W - - S	**2.45pm**	7.30am + 1	Midlander	—

85 Queen Street, Melbourne, Victoria, Australia 3000.
Telephone: (03) 608 0811. Telex: AA31109. FAX: (03) 670 8808

An association of the five government-owned Railway Systems — Australian National, Queensland Railways, the State Rail Authority of New South Wales, Public Transport Corporation — Victoria (V/Line & The Met), and Western Australian Government Railways (Westrail).

FURTHER INFORMATION IS AVAILABLE FROM:

New South Wales
The Rail Travel Centre
State Rail of NSW
Transport House
11-31 York Street
SYDNEY NSW 2000
Telephone:
Enquiries (02) 29 7614
Toll Free (008) 043 126
Bookings (02) 217 8812
Telex: AA73165

Tasmania
Tasmanian Travel Centre
8C Elizabeth Street
HOBART TAS 7000
Telephone: (002) 30 0211
Telex: AA58017

South Australia
Australian National
Travel Centre
132 North Terrace, ADELAIDE
SA 5000 (GPO Box 1743)
Telephone: (08) 231 4366
Reservations: (08) 217 4455
Telex: AA82829

Queensland
City Booking Office
Queensland Railways
208 Adelaide Street
BRISBANE QLD 4000
Telephone: (07) 235 0211
Telex: AA41514

Victoria
V/Line Travel, Transport House
589 Collins Street
MELBOURNE VIC 3000
Telephone: V/Line (03) 619 5000
Or Country Calls (Local charge only)
(008) 136 109
Reservations: (03) 619 5000
Telex: AA33801

Western Australia
Interstate Booking Office, Westrail Centre
PERTH WA 6000 (GPO S1422)
Telephone: (09) 326 2222
Telex: AA92460
Westrail Travel Centre, City Rail Station, Perth
Telephone: (09) 326 2690. Telex: WATRAV 95735

These pages: **A sampling of the modern diesel locomotives that haul the *Indian-Pacific* from province to province. Note that each of these locomotives bears the colors of its respective provincial railway.**

42217
217
4201

runs from Kalgoorlie to Perth and vice versa six days per week.

The stop here lasts one and one-half hours, allowing plenty of time to stretch the limbs. Night will have fallen as the train strikes out for Perth, allowing just one more night to have a sing-along beside the lounge piano or organ, and perhaps an opportunity to firm up friendships made en route.

The *Indian-Pacific* arrives in Perth at 7:00 on the following morning. The trip from beginning to end takes approximately 65.5 hours, or two and three-quarter days. Perth is a cosmopolitan city that is getting richer by the day on Western Australia's tremendous mineral wealth. It has an abundance of attractions, including sailing on Perth Water, an arm of the Swann River; and Tudor-styled Old London Court, a quaint shopping and tourist district.

Fremantle, just south of Perth, is the jumping-off place for oceangoing travelers to Europe. Of course, many may decide to make a return run to Sydney aboard the fabulous *Indian-Pacific*.

Above: **The cover of an *Indian-Pacific* information pamphlet. *At right:* The dramatic interior of East Perth Rail Terminal.**

WESTRAIL

The Orient Express (Venice-Simplon and Nostalgie Istanbul Orient Express)

vision was realized when the Belgian Georges Nagelmackers founded the Wagons-Lits Company in 1869. It was a vision for European train travel, and was inspired by the American George Pullman and his grand sleeping cars. Nagelmackers, having been in America for a short while, marvelled at opulence of the Pullman sleepers and the freedom that they allowed in their unobstructed travels over one private railway after another, making fast and comfortable work of long rail journeys. He was sure that Europeans could enjoy the same luxury and freedom.

A major obstacle existed to Nagelmackers' vision. The European continent of the 1860s was covered with hundreds of small, independent railway systems, each operating strictly within its own country. It was very difficult to get railways to cooperate on joint ventures, let alone countries.

Upon his return to Belgium from the US, Nagelmackers supported his dream as he worked at his vocation to that time, which was mine engineering. Despite such setbacks as the Franco-Prussian War and the

VENICE SIMPLON
ORIENT-EXPRESS
LONDON · PARIS · VENICE
CAFE
LAFAYETTE

calcified attitudes of some railway executives, Nagelmackers had convinced enough railway managers to sign short-term contracts for his cars that he founded his long-haul European sleeping car company in the autumn of 1872.

The first Nagelmackers cars were four-wheel railway carriages with Pullman-like convertible day and night accommodations. Two restrooms were tucked into the space left over, and one of these was additionally equipped with a wash basin. The cars saw service in early 1873. After a month or so of desultory public response, Nagelmackers was desperate. Just then, in mid-spring of 1873, Colonel William d'Alton Mann—an American investor looking for sleeping car business in the fresh European market—met and became Nagelmackers' partner.

Mann's money promised longevity, and the two men founded Mann's Railway Sleeping Carriage Company by summer of that same year. The cars were expanded to a six-wheel configuration, and were called 'Mann Boudoir Sleeping Cars.'

As compared with the Pullmans, which had sleeping berths in sections of an otherwise open carbody, the Mann

Previous page: **A diner and an *Orient Express* poster. *Above opposite:* Inside a classic buffet car. *At right:* Ready to board the *Venice-Simplon Orient Express*. *Above:* A sleeping car.**

vehicles' sleeping berths were enclosed in separate compartments. Some of the Mann Cars also had a separate six-berth compartment for passengers' servants.

A considerable business boost came from the publicity that attended England's Prince of Wales (later King Edward VII), in his usage of one of the cars for a trip to various nations on the Continent. This gave impetus to Nagelmackers' most cherished dream—the establishment of international through service from Paris to Vienna.

By 1874, the excitement of international sleeping car service had caught on, and the business had 40 cars in operation. In December of 1876, Nagelmackers had enough capital to buy out Mann, and immediately reformed the company as *Compagnie Internationale des Wagons-Lits et des Grands Express Européens*, or more commonly known as 'Wagons-Lits.'

The year 1880 saw the introduction of Europe's first eight-wheel sleeper with bogie trucks, an American invention that vastly improved the ride, and greatly decreased the chances of derailment. In 1881, Wagons-Lits produced its first full diner car for service between Paris and the French Riviera, and the Paris-Vienna international service had become extremely popular.

Georges Nagelmackers took his next bold step—that of convincing the railways involved with Wagons-Lits to exper-

iment with trains that were composed only of his sleeping and diner cars. This experiment was so successful that, as of October 1882, eight railway companies agreed to license an all-passenger Wagons-Lits train from Paris to (what was then) Constantinople.

The first such train ran on 5 June 1883, and was named the *Orient Express*. Special rolling stock that had been designed for the train had not been completed in time, so the train was at first a scaled-down version of the envisioned *Orient Express*. Its consist was as follows: two sleeper cars, a diner, and mail and baggage coaches. This primordial *Orient Express* ran twice per week, leaving Paris at 19:30 on Tuesdays and Fridays, and arriving, so to speak, at Constantinople at 7:00 on Fridays and Tuesdays.

On 4 October 1883, Nagelmackers and 40 dignitaries and journalists inaugurated the *Orient Express* as it should have been, with the new cars. Thus, the train and its extra-luxurious and bogie-truck-equipped cars set off on its five-day journey to Constantinople. The train was so opulent that no women were allowed to come on this first run of the sparkling new equipment: it was felt that bandits in the regions beyond the Carpathians might make an attack on so splendid a train. (Bulgarian bandits did attempt at least one raid on a twentieth-century *Orient Express*.)

The guests on this inaugural train were astonished by the luxuriousness of the train's appointments. Dinners were gala affairs that lasted well into the evening hours. At one point, a Hungarian gypsy band led by one of the best Bohemian

***At right:* Artwork featuring the *Orient Express*. *Above:* Leda and the Swan grace a restored, tiled *Orient Express* room floor.**

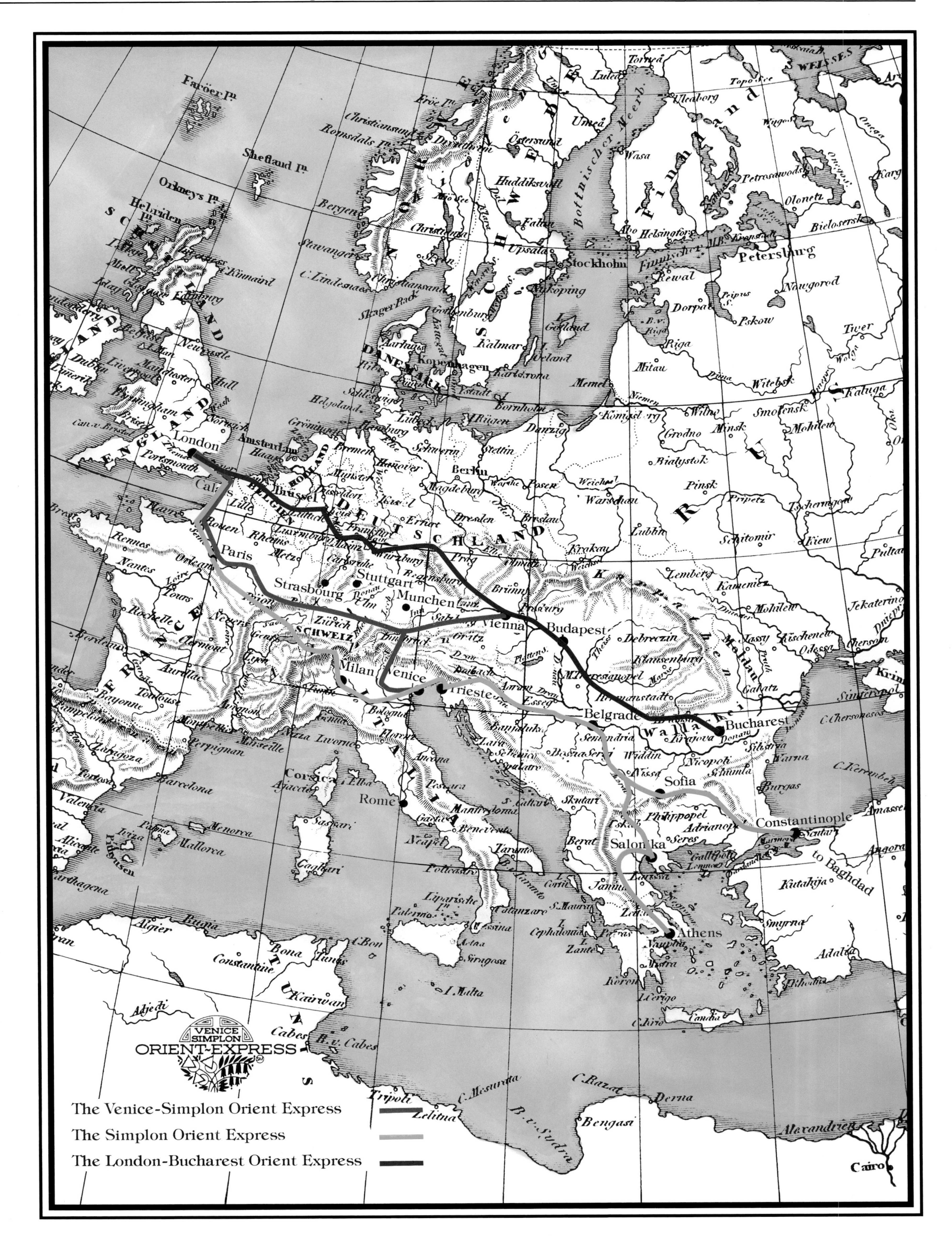
London
Calais
Paris
Strasbourg
Stuttgart
Munchen
Zürich
Vienna
Budapest
Milan
Venice
Trieste
Belgrade
Bucharest
Sofia
Constantinople
to Baghdad
Salonika
Athens
Rome
Cairo
Stockholm
Petersburg
Berlin
VENICE
SIMPLON
ORIENT-EXPRESS
The Venice-Simplon Orient Express
The Simplon Orient Express
The London-Bucharest Orient Express

1990 SCHEDULE

Please note that this schedule is for your guidance only; timings are approximate and subject to change. **The correct departure time(s) should be printed on your VSOE ticket.**
Passengers should reconfirm arrival and departure times 48 hours prior to travelling by calling the VSOE Reservation Office.
During certain months, the VSOE operates a service between London and Vienna via Salzburg, following the same route between London and Innsbruck for both destinations.
For 1990, new northbound routes have been introduced in the months of Feb, Mar, Oct and Nov, please see below for full details.
For your information, continental times shown are one hour ahead of UK time **N.B. between Sept 29 through Oct 29 add one hour to the UK times shown.**

SOUTHBOUND	MEALS	LONDON-VENICE		LONDON-VIENNA		VENICE-LONDON		VIENNA-LONDON		MEALS	NORTHBOUND
THURSDAY/SUNDAY		**ARR.**	**DEP.**	**ARR.**	**DEP.**	**ARR.**	**DEP.**	**ARR.**	**DEP.**		**WEDNESDAY/SATURDAY**
London (Victoria)			11.00		11.00		10.40			LUNCH	**Venice** (Santa Lucia)
Folkestone (Harbor)	LUNCH	12.45		12.45		12.00	12.10				Verona (Porta Nuova)
CHANNEL CROSSING									09.55		**Vienna** (Westbahnhof)
Boulogne (Maritime)			16.57		16.57			13.48	14.05	LUNCH	Salzburg (Hbf)
Paris (Gare de l'Est)	DINNER	20.37	21.33	20.37	21.33	16.35	16.55	16.36	16.55	TEA	**Innsbruck** (Hbf)
FRIDAY/MONDAY		NEXT DAY		NEXT DAY		18.35	18.43	18.35	18.45		St. Anton am Arlberg
Zürich (Flughafen)	BREAKFAST	06.29	06.47	06.29	06.47	20.22	21.00	20.22	21.00	DINNER	Buchs
Buchs		09.09	09.44	09.09	09.44	23.15	23.35	23.15	23.35		Zürich (Flughafen)
St. Anton am Arlberg		11.08	11.19	11.08	11.19	NEXT DAY		NEXT DAY			**THURSDAY/SUNDAY**
Innsbruck (Hbf)	LUNCH	12.42	13.02	12.42	13.02	09.13	09.45	09.13	09.45	BREAKFAST	**Paris** (Gare de l'Est)
Salzburg (Hbf)	TEA			16.30	16.50	13.30		13.30		BRUNCH	Boulogne (Maritime)
Vienna (Westbahnhof)				20.05							CHANNEL CROSSING
Verona (Porta Nuova)	TEA	17.06	17.15				15.55		15.55		Folkestone (Harbor)
Venice (Santa Lucia)		18.48				17.50		17.50		TEA	**London** (Victoria)

DEPARTURE DATES:

LONDON TO VENICE:
Thurdays February 22 to October 11 and November 15 (except July 12, 26/ August 9, 23).
Sundays March 4 to November 11.

LONDON TO VIENNA:
Thurdays July 12, 26/August 9, 23/ October 18, 25 and November 1, 8.

VENICE TO LONDON:
Wednesdays April 4 to October 17
Saturdays April 7 to July 7, July 21, August 4, 18 and September 1 to October 13.

VIENNA TO LONDON:
Saturdays July 14, 28 and August 11, 25.

NORTHBOUND ROUTING VARIATIONS TO PARIS AND LONDON IN SPRING AND AUTUMN

VENICE – PARIS & LONDON VIA MILAN

WEDNESDAY/SATURDAY	ARR.	DEP.
Venice		10.40
Verona	12.00	12.10
Milan	14.30	15.00
Lausanne	20.00	20.30
Paris	09.13	09.45
London	17.50	

Departure Dates: Wednesdays February 21 to March 28. Saturdays March 3 to 31.

VENICE – PARIS & LONDON VIA MUNICH

WEDNESDAY	ARR.	DEP.
Venice		10.40
Verona	12.00	12.10
Innsbruck	16.36	16.55
Munich	19.00	19.30
Paris	09.13	09.45
London	17.50	

Departure Dates: Wednesdays October 24 to November 14.

VIENNA – PARIS & LONDON VIA MUNICH

SATURDAY	ARR.	DEP.
Vienna		11.55
Salzburg	15.48	16.05
Munich	19.00	19.30
Paris	09.13	09.45
London	17.50	

Departure Dates: Saturdays October 20 to November 10.

25

violinists came aboard and gave a two-and-one-half-hour concert. A bit farther down the line, the King of Rumania invited them to a feast at his summer palace. The debut of *Orient Express* luxury was a smashing success.

Up until 1888, however, passengers had to debark at Giurgiu, Romania for a ferry across the Danube to Rustchuk, Bulgaria. From there, a Bulgarian railway allowed them to proceed to Varna, on the Black Sea, where they boarded an Austrian Lloyd ocean liner bound for Constantinople.

The reason for this discontinuity was Russia's determination to protect is own shipping business in the region. Hence, Russian emissaries had blocked efforts to build a direct rail line to the Turkish capital. However, pro-railway forces eventually prevailed, and rails through to Constantinople were completed in the winter of 1888. With through rail service established, the *Orient Express* left Paris at 19:30 Wednesday, and 10 railways and six countries later, arrived in Constantinople at 17:35 on Saturday. The distance travelled was 2970 km (1857 miles).

This original line ran via Bucharest, but an improved line was developed that went by way of Belgrade, whereupon a connecting train ran twice weekly from Vienna to Bucharest. The train that ran this latter route, Paris-Vienna-Bucharest, was the train that longest carried the name *Orient Express*, surviving into the 1980s. With a travelling time of 36 hours and 10 minutes, the train left Paris nightly at

Previous pages: **Lunch aboard.** ***At right:*** **Clientele.** ***Opposite, left and right:*** **An armoire and a water-closet; and a berth.**

1990 VENICE SIMPLON-ORIENT-EXPRESS TRAIN ONLY PRICES

OVERNIGHT TRAVEL ON THE VENICE SIMPLON-ORIENT-EXPRESS

SOUTHBOUND	Feb 22-Mar 31	Apr 1-Nov 15	NORTHBOUND	Feb 21-Mar 31	Apr 1-Nov 14
	US$	US$		US$	US$
London-Venice/Vienna/Salzburg	1190	1300	Venice/Vienna/Salzburg-London	1100	1300
London-Innsbruck	1080	1190	Innsbruck-London	–	1190
London-Zürich/St. Anton	970	1080	St. Anton/Zürich/Munich-London	–	1080
			Venice/Vienna/Salzburg-Paris	990	1190
Paris-Venice/Vienna/Salzburg	1100	1190	Innsbruck-Paris	–	1080
Paris-Innsbruck	990	1080	St. Anton/Zürich/Munich-Paris	–	970
Paris-Zürich/St. Anton	880	970	Milan/Lausanne-London	1020	–
			Milan/Lausanne-Paris	910	–

DAYTIME TRAVEL ON THE VENICE SIMPLON-ORIENT-EXPRESS

SOUTHBOUND	Feb 22-Mar 31	Apr 1-Nov 15	NORTHBOUND	Feb 21-Mar 31	Apr 1-Nov 14
DAY CAR ACCOMMODATION†	US$	US$	**DAY CAR ACCOMMODATION†**	US$	US$
London-Paris	425	590	Paris-London	380	425
Zürich-Venice/Vienna/Salzburg	425	590	Venice/Vie/Salzburg-Munich/Zürich	380	425
Zürich-Innsbruck	245	410	Innsbruck-Zürich	–	410
Innsbruck-Venice/Vienna/Salzburg	245	410	Venice/Vienna/Salzburg-Innsbruck	–	410
			Venice-Lausanne	245	–
CABIN ACCOMMODATION	US$	US$	**CABIN ACCOMMODATION**	US$	US$
London-Paris	560	700	Paris-London	500	560
Zürich-Venice/Vienna/Salzburg	560	700	Venice/Vie/Salzburg-Munich/Zürich	500	560
Zürich-Innsbruck	380	520	Innsbruck-Zürich	–	520
Innsbruck-Venice/Vienna/Salzburg	380	520	Venice/Vienna/Salzburg-Innsbruck	–	520
			Venice-Lausanne	380	–

SUPPLEMENTS TO ABOVE PRICES ON OVERNIGHT TRAVEL

SOUTHBOUND	US$	US$	NORTHBOUND	US$	US$
Single Cabin	220	220	Single Cabin	220	220
Double Cabin for Single Occupancy	825	975	Double Cabin for Single Occupancy	825	975
Cabin-Suite*	1650	1950	Cabin-Suite*	1650	1950
Each Stopover	160	160	One Stopover	No charge	No charge

ADDITIONAL INFORMATION:
1. The above prices are per person in shared double cabin and include all table d'hôte meals and tax while aboard the Venice Simplon-Orient-Express.
2. There is a 25% reduction on overnight travel in both directions.
3. There is a 10% reduction on day sector travel in both directions and a 10% reduction on overnight travel in one direction, day sector the other direction.
4. There is a 50% reduction on children 12 and under travelling with an adult and sharing a double cabin.
5. July and August northbound, children travel FREE (one child berth free for each accompanying adult, double berth cabins only).

† Day car accommodation includes all meals on the VSOE but not private cabin facilities. Passengers are allocated reserved seats in one of the restaurant cars for the journey.

* Cabin-Suite accommodation provides private use of a second cabin (available for overnight sectors only). Wait list cabin-suites are available within 7 weeks of departure date at a reduced rate of $550 (Feb 21-Mar 31) and $650 (Apr 1-Nov 15). Please request to be wait listed, if required, at the time of booking.

Please note that only one reduction per person applies.

ALL THAT REMAINS IS TO MAKE IT HAPPEN.
See your travel agent or call our reservations desk at:

Venice Simplon-Orient-Express
One World Trade Center, Suite 2565, New York, NY 10048

For reservations on the Venice Simplon-Orient-Express train and m.v. 'Orient Express' cruise ship call:-
(800) 524-2420 (Nationwide) (212) 938-6830 (New York State) (800) 451-2253 (Canada)
Sabre Access:-Y/OTH/OEX

For reservations at our 8 hotels listed on pages 20/21 call:-
(800) 237-1236 (Nationwide) (212) 839-0222 (New York State) (800) 451-2253 (Canada)
Telex:- WUD 981453 (VSOE NYK)

CONDITIONS OF CARRIAGE FOR INCLUSIVE ARRANGEMENT BOOKINGS

Inclusive Arrangements are defined as holidays combining VSOE train travel with one or more of the following elements: hotel accommodation / air / m.v. 'Orient-Express' cruise journey, arranged by the Venice Simplon-Orient-Express. VSOE are not able to book confirmed flights, hotel accommodation or the m.v. 'Orient-Express' cruise until a deposit or full payment is received.

Conditions for Inclusive Arrangements: In addition to the Conditions of Carriage and the Convention referred to in point 1 of the Booking and Carriage Conditions and Limitations all bookings for Inclusive Arrangements are subject to the following conditions; (i) as regards any part of the carriage which is performed by an airline, the conditions of carriage of that airline and any conventions or other regulations incorporated therein, (ii) as regards any hotel occupancy arranged by the Company, the conditions of occupancy (if any) of the relevant hotel, (iii) as regards any part of the carriage by sea, the Conditions of Carriage of Sealink UK Limited and the provisions of the Athens Convention (which may also be applicable) and (iv) as regards any transfer service, the conditions (if any) of the transfer operator.

Copies of these conditions can be obtained from the relevant airline, hotel, Sealink UK Limited or transfer companies. All the Booking Conditions and Procedures set out above and contained within this brochure apply insofar as they are relevant to the holidays and references to 'the fare' shall mean the holiday price, references to 'the journey' shall mean the holiday.

Changes to a Confirmed Booking: (for Inclusive Arrangement bookings). Any change to a confirmed booking for an Inclusive Arrangement will subject each passenger to a charge of $25.

Cancellations: (for Inclusive Arrangement bookings). Cancellation charges shall be made by the Company on cancellation to bookings on inclusive arrangements as per point 10(b) of the Booking and Carriage Conditions and Limitations.

Surcharges: Prices shown in this brochure are based on known costs and exchange rates as at April 17th, 1989, which exchange rates are available from the VSOE Reservation Office.

In respect of air travel, hotel occupancy, m.v. 'Orient-Express' cruise and transfer service comprised in any Inclusive Arrangement, the Company reserves the right to impose a surcharge on the inclusive tour price of such an amount as will in the reasonable opinion of the Company compensate the Company for any adverse movement in relevant currency exchange rates. Any such surcharge may be imposed and shall be payable at any time prior to the commencement date of the holiday.

26

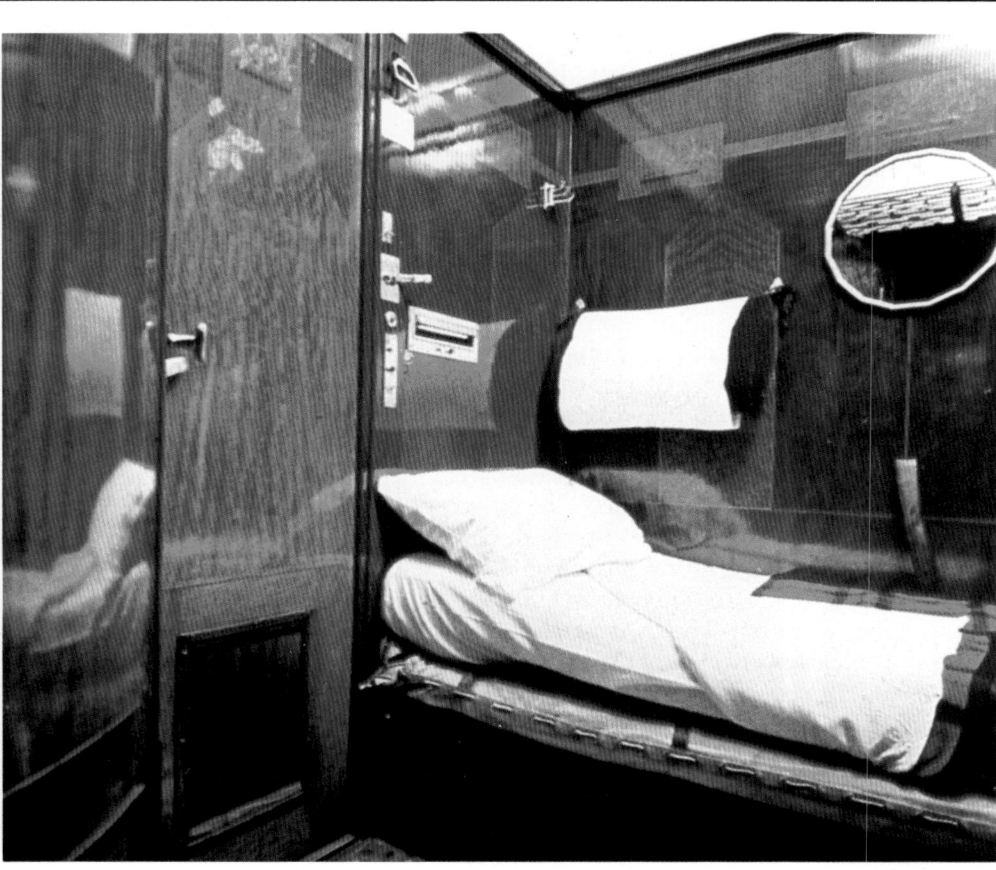

23:35 and arrived in Bucharest at 11:45 on the third day, with an average speed of 68 kph (42 mph) for 2448 km (1530 miles).

The Simplon Tunnel was opened in 1906, connecting rails between Switzerland and Italy. This gave rise to a service that rivalled the original *Orient Express* route for popularity, and was named the *Simplon Orient Express*, beginning at Paris, and going via Switzerland, Italy, Austria, Serbia (Yugoslavia), Bulgaria and Turkey to Constantinople.

All *Orient Express* service was discontinued at the outbreak of World War I, and was revived for one year in 1919, including a luxury train for military chiefs of staff, on a Paris-Vienna-Warsaw itinerary. That same year, the Paris to Constantinople itinerary was completely taken over by the *Simplon Orient Express*. The *Orient Express* in most of its forms then disappeared, but in 1921, it was once more doing regular business on a variety of international routes, and in fact, was entering its legendary prime—the 'golden years' between World War I and World War II.

As can be expected, *Orient Express* passengers were likely to be of the upper classes—royalty, government officials, high-ranking military officers, tycoons and, in general, the well-to-do with business or pleasure of any kind to conduct on any one of the train's many routes.

There were many tales linking the *Orient Express* with secret missions, spectacular romances and extraordinary occurrences of all sorts. However, as one 'King's Messenger' (British Foreign Office diplomat) said, 'the Greyhound knows his business far too well for dalliance.' Another such personage said, in commenting on the supposed *femmes fatale* of the *Orient Express*, 'I have never seen them.'

However, even the following partial list of notable *Orient Express* passengers is sure to stimulate the imagination. Passengers included the Austro-Hungarian Emperor and Empress Charles and Elizabeth; the Bulgarian kings Ferdinand and Boris; Edward, the Prince of Wales, formerly Edward VIII, and his wife, Wallis Ward Simpson, for whom he had abdicated the English throne; the Duke and Duchess of

At top: **A Nord Railway 4-6-2 ferries a *Simplon Express* sleeping car from Paris to Calais. *Above:* A typical turn-of-the century European luxury train. *At right:* An early luxury salon car.**

ALARM SIGNAL

SBB

York, who later became King George VI and Queen Elizabeth of England; King Carol II of Romania; Mata Hari, the infamous spy; and Lord Baden-Powell, founder of the Boy Scouts.

The interior appointments of the cars soon emerged from the styles of the turn of the century to a highly tasteful form of Art Deco in the 1920s. Mahogany and walnut wall paneling, with fine inlay work, formed the base for the interior decor of the cars. The exteriors were elegant, with a blue and white color scheme that hinted at royalty, and was distinctive, with large, golden medallions emblazoned on the cars' sides.

Inside, rich marquetry work on finely-finished wood panels, brass fixtures and ornate upholstery greeted the boarding passenger. Amid a veritable animated fashion plate of stylishly dressed men, women and children making themselves comfortable for the journey, an attentive, but not obsequious, steward saw to it that all baggage was properly stowed.

Tables in the diner bore sparkling silverware, and were accustomed to bearing sumptuous meals. Pampered travellers sat amid mahogany and brass, leaning back into the rich velour of their chairs. Pristine tablecloths held an assortment of crystal and silver that made the diner almost more a display case than a place for eating food. The lights in some cars were elegant brass goosenecks coming out from the wall, with frosted glass shades in the form of small, half-open tulips.

While food had to be loaded afresh at every border, the quality of the food was as good as could be found in the finest restaurants. With a fully-equipped kitchen and a

Above: **An 1888 poster for the *Orient Express*. *At left:* A Swiss electric locomotive heads the *Nostalgie Orient Express* in 1984.**

battery of gourmet chefs, *Orient Express* diner cars were dedicated to serving the tastes of a clientele who, for the most part, knew and appreciated high cuisine as an everyday occurrence.

Passenger cabins were of 1920s opulence—superb wood paneling, with little art deco motifs tastefully highlighting the gleaming, deep-grained surface. The windows were large, and closets were capacious enough to hold all the clothing that was needed. This was important for a journey on a train that required formal evening wear at dinner, and nothing less than elegance at all other times. Many of these compartments had their own wash stand, with hot and cold water, in a stow-away cabinet. There was a mosaic-tile-floored water closet at either end of each sleeping car, with shower facilities available for long-haul journeys.

If passengers began their trip at Paris, they pulled out from the Gare de Lyon, that incredible rococo palace of a station that was built for the Paris Exhibition of 1900. The cavernous but astonishingly balanced excesses of this station were designed as more than just an architectural paean to the Third Empire, they created an experience that conveyed the very essence of another place and time.

Agatha Christie conveys some sense of the *Orient Express* in her famous detective tale, *Murder on the Orient Express*. Of a morning, you could have room service deliver fresh breakfast buns and coffee, or tea. There was, also, some variation in the decor of the trains, as they were designed individually by the greatest designers of the day. Detail, but not quality, varied. Perhaps one train might have recessed lighting, while another might have brass goose-necked lamps; one might have tufted leather seats, while another had seats of rich velour. Great pride was taken in the decor of each train, but some features were universally *Orient Express* features: the rich wood panelling with intricate inlay work, and the beautiful brass lamps that adorned tables here and there throughout the train.

The *Orient Express* routing system went through a great number of permutations over the years, especially in the train's 'classic' period—between the First and Second world wars, when travellers could take the *Simplon Orient Express* to Constantinople/Istanbul (that city's name was changed in 1930), the *London-Bucharest Orient Express* or the *Ostende-Vienna Orient Express* as far as Budapest for a connection to Constantinople/Istanbul, where they then crossed the Bosphorus for further travel to Baghdad, Tehran and Tripoli (and, by extension, to Cairo).

There were, for example, at least six routes extant in the 1930s. In addition to those mentioned above, there were the *London-Bucharest-Istanbul Orient Express* and the *Arlberg Orient Express*. Passengers starting from London took the ferry across the English Channel to Calais, where they resumed train travel. The London-Bucharest route, for instance, began at London, crossed the Channel and proceeded on via Ostende, Liège, Cologne and Frankfurt, before jogging sharply east into Czechoslovakia for a stop at Karlovy Vary, then swinging back westward to Vienna, and from thence to Budapest and Bucharest.

The *Simplon Orient Express* took a route that cut through western Europe for the most part. Beginning at London, one crossed the Channel to Boulogne, and thence to Paris, Lausanne, Milan, Venice, Trieste, Postojna, Vincovki and Niš. At Niš, passengers had a choice of routes, one of which went the traditional way through Sofia and Svilengrad to Constantinople/Istanbul; the other route took them through Skoplje and Salonika to Athens.

Therefore, European travellers had availed to them, while travelling in the utmost luxury, most of the leading cities in Europe. More northern travellers relied upon the special

Above right: **Luncheon on the *Venice-Simplon Orient Express*.**
At right: **Dinner aboard the *Venice-Simplon Orient Express*.**
Above opposite: **Fond farewell on the *Venice-Simplon Orient Express*.**

services of the *Nord Express*. Of course, there were also the *Sud Express*, the *Fleche d'Or*, the *Flying Scotsman* and other great luxury trains to expand their travel itineraries on the Continent and in Great Britain.

Operations within the *Orient Express* routings further increased the travel options for passengers. For example, the *Simplon Orient Express* picked up the central part of its consist—sleepers bound for Constantinople/Istanbul, Athens and Bucharest—at Paris. At that point, the train would be composed of five sleeping cars, a diner and a baggage-mail car that also included a small shower facility. At Milan, the diner crew was replaced by fresh personnel, and at Vinkovci, two sleepers bound for Bucharest were left off the train to make their connection to one of the Bucharest-bound trains.

From Vinkovci, the *Simplon Orient Express* proceeded to Belgrade, where it rendezvoused with various of the other *Orient Express* trains, to take on additional sleepers from Berlin, Ostend, Amsterdam or Prague. Thence on to Nis, where sleepers bound for Athens were detached for an Athens-bound train. In the 1920s, the diner was detached at the Bulgarian border, but in the 1930s, it remained with the train all the way to Istanbul.

As for the above-mentioned service through to Baghdad, Tehran and Tripoli, Wagons-Lits was granted a contract to extend its service through to the Middle East in 1926. In 1930, the special service was inaugurated as the *Taurus Express*. At Constantinople/Istanbul, passengers debarked from the *Simplon Orient Express* for a ferry across the Bosphorus, which took them to Haydarpasa, where the *Taurus Express*, with an all-new diner and sleeping cars, awaited them. The *Taurus Express* offered two routes.

One of these was the 'Baghdad' route, and went as far as the Iraqi border at Tel Kotchek, where passengers transferred to an Iraqi Railways train: the track gauge was eventually standardized, allowing through travel to Baghdad, and from thence, on a roundabout route to Tehran, in 1940. The other route, to Tripoli, got you as far as that Lebanese city on the *Taurus Express*. By extension, however, passengers could go all the way to Cairo. From Tripoli, travellers boarded a bus to Haifa, and from there, boarded a Wagons-Lits deluxe train to the Suez Canal. A ferry across the canal connected with an Egyptian Pullman train to Cairo.

Orient Express service was suspended during World War II, and was restored afterward, though through service was disturbed on the *Simplon Orient Express* by the outbreak of civil war in Greece. Passengers debarked the train in Bulgaria, near the Grecian border, boarded a bus or a truck for the ride through the Grecian province of Thrace, and boarded an *Orient Express* train once more in Turkey. While full service was restored in 1949, terrorist activities caused the railroads to take precautions.

In fact, one late-1940s *Simplon Orient Express* train was specially outfitted for the short haul through Thrace. Five empty freight cars were coupled in front of the locomotive, to explode any mines that might be set; immediately behind the locomotive were five Turkish railroad cars, followed by the *Orient Express* dining car and sleepers; behind these were several coaches full of battle-ready soldiers; and bringing up the rear was a flatcar bearing an armored car that was equipped with a cannon.

Whatever route was taken, the always memorable European countryside and striking cityscapes flashed past the windows. The sights and attractions of London are too well-documented to record here, and as one approached the English coast, the gently verdant Kentish landscape

Above: **A 1920s luxury train poster.** ***Above right:*** **A cabin view of an Intraflug** ***Orient Express*** **train.** ***At right:*** **A salon.** ***Above opposite: Nostalgie Istanbul Orient Express*** **art.**

rolled past in soothing visual rhythms. Across the Channel lay Paris—like London, a legendary city.

Lush forests, verdant fields, the cold, imperious majesty of the Alps and more lay beyond the car windows. Grand country villas, castles and monumental fortresses dotted the countryside. Country villages and towns lay here and there, like counterpoints to both natural and urban splendors. The numerous routings of the *Orient Express* made for a train system that could bring the traveller to the very best Europe had to offer.

Also rolling past in an unforgettable pastiche of ancient and modern history were such European cities as Zurich, at the end of pristine Lake Zurich, with the University of Zurich, and the two late-Medieval churches, Gross Munster and Frau Munster; Vienna, once the crown jewel of all Europe, seated on the south bank of the legendary Danube River, with its Classical, Gothic and Renaissance architecture, opera and famous Spanish Riding School; Budapest, where history united two villages, Buda and Pest, to form one of the historically powerful capitals of Europe; and, of course, the River Danube itself, the very heart of Europe, decisive in so much history that it has helped to build as well as destroy the sovereignty of nations.

Then, situated in the luxurious confines of their ultra-comfortable train, *Orient Express* passengers noted a subtle change in the scenery as the train rolled on southward. First there was the warmly bucolic countryside of Yugoslavia. Then, in the waning light of the day, the increasingly dry and Mediterranean countryside of Bulgaria.

Here was Sofia, the Bulgarian capital, whose name means 'Wisdom,' set upon a plateau between the Balkans and the Rhodope Mountains. This city which began as a first-century Roman spa, now commands the trade routes to Belgrade, Macedonia, the Danube and Istanbul.

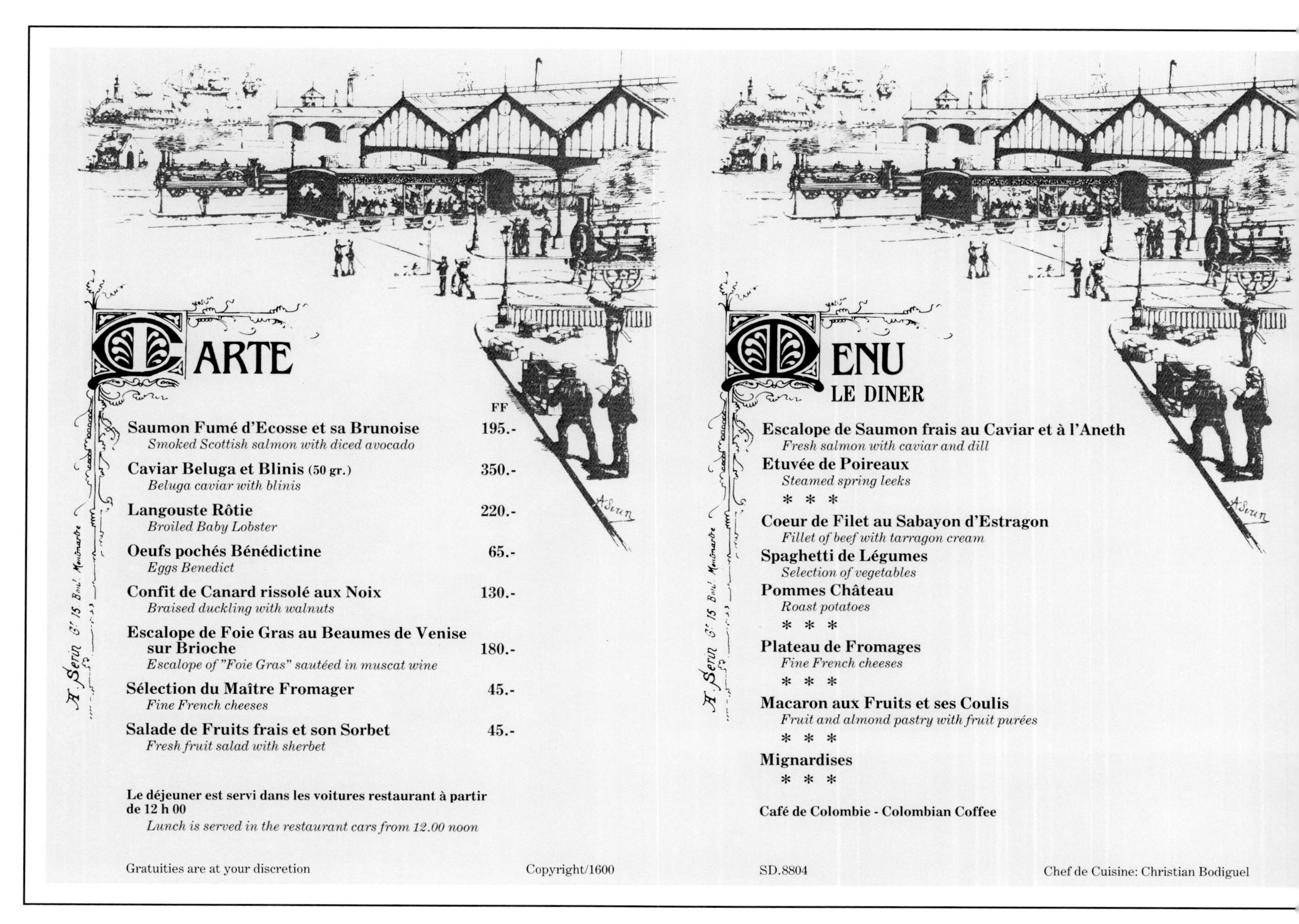

CARTE

	FF
Saumon Fumé d'Ecosse et sa Brunoise *Smoked Scottish salmon with diced avocado*	195.-
Caviar Beluga et Blinis (50 gr.) *Beluga caviar with blinis*	350.-
Langouste Rôtie *Broiled Baby Lobster*	220.-
Oeufs pochés Bénédictine *Eggs Benedict*	65.-
Confit de Canard rissolé aux Noix *Braised duckling with walnuts*	130.-
Escalope de Foie Gras au Beaumes de Venise sur Brioche *Escalope of "Foie Gras" sautéed in muscat wine*	180.-
Sélection du Maître Fromager *Fine French cheeses*	45.-
Salade de Fruits frais et son Sorbet *Fresh fruit salad with sherbet*	45.-

Le déjeuner est servi dans les voitures restaurant à partir de 12 h 00
Lunch is served in the restaurant cars from 12.00 noon

Gratuities are at your discretion

Copyright/1600

MENU
LE DINER

Escalope de Saumon frais au Caviar et à l'Aneth
Fresh salmon with caviar and dill
Etuvée de Poireaux
Steamed spring leeks
* * *
Coeur de Filet au Sabayon d'Estragon
Fillet of beef with tarragon cream
Spaghetti de Légumes
Selection of vegetables
Pommes Château
Roast potatoes
* * *
Plateau de Fromages
Fine French cheeses
* * *
Macaron aux Fruits et ses Coulis
Fruit and almond pastry with fruit purées
* * *
Mignardises
* * *

Café de Colombie - Colombian Coffee

SD.8804

Chef de Cuisine: Christian Bodiguel

The first glimpse of minarets as the sun rose informed *Orient Express* passengers that they were nearing their classic destination, that city on the banks of the Bosphorus—and then, at 8:30, they were there. Istanbul commands the narrow Bosphorus between the Black Sea and the Mediterranean, and hence has been of strategic importance for literally thousands of years. The Greeks first settled it in 667 BC, calling it Byzantium.

It was here that the Roman Emperor Constantine declared Christianity to be legal, and set up the capital of the Eastern Roman Empire, naming it Constantinople. The city prospered with unprecedented wealth and learning for the better part of 1000 years as the queen city of the world during the Middle Ages, and was the seat of an empire as large as Rome at its height.

The massive sixth-century church, Hagia Sophia, still dominates the city's skyline with its huge central dome, though it has been made into a mosque, and its brilliant interior mosaics have been plastered over by the Moslems, who invaded the eviscerated city, after its decline, in the fifteenth century. Renamed Istanbul in 1930, it is still an important trading port, and is redolent with fascinating history.

Such was travel in the 'golden age' of the *Orient Express.* Later trains such as the *Direct Orient* were much-reduced imitations of the splendid equipage and service that reached its height in the 1920s and 1930s. Ordinary coaches had replaced many of the original cars, and through-coach and diner service was cut back. The proliferation of routings was also diminished. The *Direct Orient Express* was removed

At right: **A sumptuous table setting aboard the *Venice-Simplon Orient Express.* *Opposite:* Inside another restored diner.**

CARTE DES VINS

VENICE SIMPLON ORIENT-EXPRESS

VINS BLANCS

	FF 1/2	FF 1/1
BORDEAUX		
Sauternes Cruse	95	170.-
CHÂTEAU D'YQUEM GRAND CRU 1981		950.-
BOURGOGNES		
Mâcon Villages 1986		160.-
Chablis 1er Cru 1986	115	210.-
Pouilly Fuissé 1985		260.-
Meursault 1985		290.-
LOIRE		
Sancerre Bouchard 1986	90	160.-
RHONE		
MUSCAT DE BEAUMES DE VENISE	140	
PIEMONT		
Gavi de' Gavi - Tenuta La Scolca 1986		240.-
CHAMPAGNES		
Lechère Cuvée Venice Simplon-Orient-Express 1er Cru	180	360.-
Lechère Cuvée Venice Simplon-Orient-Express 1er Cru Rosé		490.-
Krug Vintage 1979		660.-
Dom Pérignon 1980		720.-
ROEDERER CRISTAL 1981 (stock limité)		910.-

Gratuities are at your discretion

VINS ROUGES

	FF 1/2	FF 1/1
BORDEAUX		
Château Bel Air *Haut-Médoc* 1983	95	170.-
Château de Lamarque *Haut-Médoc* 1982		190.-
Château La Tour de Marbuzet *St. Estèphe* 1980		190.-
Château J. Faure Grand Cru *St. Emilion* 1981		240.-
Château de Sales Grand Cru *Pomerol* 1980		360.-
Château Beychevelle *Saint Julien* 1982		620.-
CHÂTEAU BRANE CANTENAC *Margaux* 1978		830.-
BOURGOGNES		
Chassagne Montrachet 1985		220.-
Pommard 1984		370.-
Clos Vougeot Château de la Tour 1982		520.-
CORTON RENARDES 1978		780.-
BEAUJOLAIS		
Brouilly Château de Corcelles 1985	95	170.-
RHONE		
Châteauneuf-du-Pape *Domaine de Mont-Redon* 1985		160.-
Tavel Rosé	60	100.-
PIEMONT		
Barbaresco Costa Russi Gaja 1982		450.-
TOSCANE		
Brunello di Montalcino Biondi Santi 1981		340.-

8804

These pages: **As per *Orient Express* tradition, the restored Intraflug trains are hauled by the national railway of each country they pass through. Vintage steam power is used wherever possible. Therefore, *Nostalgie Istanbul Orient Express* passengers may yet thrill to Turkish steam power such as this.**

from service in May of 1977, whereupon only the old Paris-Bucharest route, via Strasbourg, Munich, Vienna and Budapest, remained. Moreover, the impoverished trains that ran this route only barely resembled the *Orient Express* that made rail travelers dream.

In 1976, the Swiss Federal Railway made a farewell gesture to the disappearing legend, and organized a successful round-trip run of a train from Zurich to Istanbul. This train was composed of Wagons-Lits cars from the heyday of European luxury train service. This gesture pulled in a surprising amount of business, but neither the railway nor Wagons-Lits wanted to carry it any further.

Aby Glatt and his associates at Intraflug AG, airline charterers located in Zurich, saw what they felt to be a priceless tradition disappearing forever. They felt that a luxurious, long-haul international train in the mold of the *Orient Express* trains of the 1920s and 1930s would still attract plenty of business, on a regular and semi-regular operations basis.

Thereupon Intraflug attempted to set up arrangements with several railways that still owned vintage luxury cars. These organizations demurred, and there was no choice but to go into the business of purchasing some of Europe's most luxurious 1920s–30s-era passenger cars. It was a true feat of collecting. At first, some of the cars used were on lease from Wagons-Lits. Also, Glatt purchased some cars at a much-heralded auction held at Monte Carlo by the renowned Sothebys firm in 1977.

All of the cars collected by Intraflug AG were built in the years between 1926 and 1929, and were originally outfitted

***At right:* Luggage tags. *Above:* Dinner on the *Nostalgie Orient Express*. Views of the original *Orient Express—opposite, top to bottom:* A diner car; interior views; mealtime in the diner.**

COMPAGNIE INTERNATIONALE DES WAGONS LITS
Nº 151 D
DINING CAR
WAGON RESTAURANT

by the finest Art Deco artists in the world. The cars have been renovated down to the charcoal heaters that provide hot water. Where parts were missing, Glatt and associates commissioned exact replicas—including precise copies of the original *Orient Express* table lamps.

Keeping up the tradition of the *Orient Express*, on-board service was to include full gourmet meals of two classes—either one of which would do credit to the finest restaurants—room service, shower facilities for long-haul travel and full salon-bar service. Very chic stationery and envelopes, bearing the train's letterhead, were made available for prestige-conscious passengers.

Intraflug soon made arrangements with various railways to begin running some of the *Orient Express* schedules of the service's heyday. In the late 1970s and early 1980s, the *Nostalgie Orient Express*, as the Intraflug train was then named, made five to six runs per year, and the most frequently followed route then was that of the old *Arlberg Orient Express*, from Zurich to Istanbul via Buchs, the Arlberg Tunnel, Innsbruck, Ljubliana, Belgrade and Sofia and back for a round trip.

On occasion, the *Nostalgie Orient Express* followed the *Simplon Orient* route to Athens. In 1978 plans were being made to include Baghdad on an itinerary, and in 1979, a round trip tour of Scandinavia was undertaken. Currently, there are several *Orient Express* route trains being run. The

Above: **The *Venice-Simplon Orient Express* winds through Austria. *Opposite:* A Turkish steam locomotive awaits the *Nostalgie Orient Express* at Edirne. *At right:* A refurbished salon car.**

TCDD
46018

03 12

Nostalgie Orient Express has had a name change to *Nostalgie Istanbul Orient Express*, and runs a route that approximates several of the classic *Orient Express* routes. One itinerary is, for example: Zurich, Munich, Salzburg, Vienna, Budapest, Sofia, Kapikule, Edirne and Istanbul. This includes a gala reception and ball in Salzburg, city tours and sightseeing in Vienna and Budapest, a gala on-board dinner (over and above the regular, sumptuous menu) and sightseeing in Sofia, Kapikule and Edirne. This train runs a regular schedule twice per year, and the journey takes four days, beginning on the morning of the first day and ending on the evening of the fourth. South to north trips are also run, with the duration being about the same.

An opera and ballet excursion train, the *Semper Opera*, also runs from Zurich to Dresden, with concert stops along the way, and a two-night extravaganza of opera and ballet at Dresden's fabulous Semper Opera. In addition to this, day trips from Zurich to Salzburg (return by nostalgic refurbished DC-3 airliner); or from Zurich to Interlaken, where passengers make a connection with the legendary Jungfrau Railways for an Alpine trip to 'the top of Europe' are also available.

The *Venice-Simplon Orient Express* is an Intraflug train that is designed to emulate the first part of the route of the old *Simplon Orient Express*. This train runs southbound five times per year, and northbound just once. The itinerary, depending upon point of boarding, begins in either London or Paris, and there is day-car accommodation that picks up and deposits passengers along the route. The full north-south itinerary for this train is, however: London, Boulogne (via Folkstone Ferry), Paris, Zurich, St Anton Am Arlberg, Innsbruck, Verona and Venice—or, as an alternate connection at Innsbruck, Salzburg and Vienna.

This train departs London at approximately 11:00 on Thursdays and Sundays, arriving in Venice at 18:50 on Fridays or Mondays, or in Vienna at 20:05 on Fridays or Mondays. The schedule is set such that, during certain months, the train makes these trips once weekly, with Thursdays and Sundays varying as the departure days. Northbound runs alternate Wednesdays and Saturdays as departure days.

In general, the *Nostalgie Istanbul* and *Venice-Simplon Orient Express* trains have been painstakingly put together from the original luxury cars that had been used on such vintage luxury trains as the fabled *Train Bleu*, the all-Pullman *Côte d'Azur*, the *Sud Express* and the *Fleche d'Or*. Many of them were unique in their interior schemes, and this uniqueness has been maintained, with the restoration of wood panelling and so forth. However, little touches have been added here and there to incorporate them into the *Orient Express* mold, such as the blue and white exterior color scheme, with the large, brass Wagons-Lits emblems blazing forth on the car sides.

There is, for instance, a salon car with tufted leather seats and the kind of recessed lighting that was popular in the Art Deco-crazed 1920–30s. A shower car that had been

At left: **Bulgarian steam locomotives like this hauled the *Orient Express* trains of 1940–73. *Above:* A classic postcard.**

specially outfitted for Milan's La Scala opera company while on tour is the only car currently in use that does not have fine wood paneling. Lavatories in many cars have tiled floors with either mythic motifs or the train's insignia emblazoned on them in fine mosaic.

Lawrence Durrell no doubt highly appreciated the original *Orient Express*, and would have loved to ride this resurrected version. One diner was the official car of the French President, from the 1890s to World War II, with the Presidential banquet table lovingly refurbished and serving regally for the repasts of modern-day rail travellers. Other diners are replete with more private accommodations, including cozy tables for two or four.

An on-board dinner, prepared by the gourmet chefs in the diner car's full kitchen (which features the original cooking equipment) might consist of four courses: filet of sole with saffron and caviar, with a watercress hollandaise sauce on the side; beef tournedos in red wine, with vegetables and roast potatoes; a fruit charlotte; and candied truffles, plus, of course, aperitifs, liqueurs and wines. Dinner is not the only opulent meal on board: luncheon, for example, might consist of medallions of beef, with a number of gourmet appetizers and desserts, plus the finest beverages.

Sleeping accommodations are two-bed compartments, convertible for day use, with wash stand and closet, opulently outfitted in fine wood and inlay work; lockable, connecting doors can turn two of these into connecting suites. At least one salon car features a baby grand piano. Passengers have a splendid chance for conviviality, with the tinkling piano in the background, and friendly voices all around. A full bar of the finest beverages further encourages a relaxed atmosphere.

Clothing worn during travel is encouraged toward the casual but smart during day, and dinner wear begins at the coat-and-tie/full dress level and escalates to the formal, in keeping with the enjoyably heightened atmosphere aboard.

This mode of travel is for those seeking civilized enjoyment. With the same end in mind, but with a much-expanded itinerary, is the Intraflug extravaganza that is run as the *Transiberian Special and Peking Orient Express*. The itinerary for this spectacular journey utilizes the best Russian and Chinese deluxe coaches. All passenger compartments have private shower and/or bath, and the trip includes cultural programs, sightseeing excursions and other items of interest along the way. The *Transiberian Special* itinerary follows the classical Trans-Siberian Railway (see the text chapter on the *Trans-Siberian Express*), swinging south at Ulan Ude for the trip to the Chinese border via Ulan Bator. At the border, a transfer of trains is made for the *Peking Orient Express* segment of the trip, and a little over a day later, passengers arrive in Peking.

This itinerary is wisely tempered with a combination of several one- to two-day overnight stints on the train and luxurious hotel stays that are part of the package's cultural and tourism program. The journey is rounded out with a cultural tour of Peking and a gala farewell dinner. All in all, this once-in-a-lifetime experience begins with an overnight stay and cultural program in Moscow and ends with the same in Peking, 17 days later. In 1988, an Intraflug train running an extension of this route—from Paris, via Germany, Poland, Russia and China to Hong Kong—executed the longest continuous rail trip on record.

Intraflug's resurrected *Orient Express* trains and their cousins also include the *American-European Express*, for which see the chapter of this text on that train. All of these trains are available for charter, with the customer's choice of cars, itinerary (to some extent) and train makeup from available stock.

At right, top to bottom: **A *Venice-Simplon Orient Express* postcard; the *Nostalgie Orient Express*; a *Venice-Simplon Orient Express* salon car; conviviality in the salon. *Opposite:* Turkish steam power evokes the glory of the old *Orient Express*.**

46052

The USSR's Trans-Siberian Express

Proven by the harsh test of history, the ***Trans-Siberian Express*** *traverses the Trans-Siberian Railway, the longest rail line in the world. The currently-used trackage from Moscow to Vladivostok totals 9297 km (5777 miles). Construction of the Trans-Siberian Railway was begun in 1891. Though its fame has come from its famous passenger train, the motivation for building the line lay in its strategic value. It was seen that a trans-Siberian rail line would help Russia consolidate its holdings in Siberia by encouraging Russian settlement there, and would greatly facilitate the maintenance of army strongholds in the east, as well as the Russian naval fleet in the Pacific.*

The construction of the Trans-Siberian Railway was begun at both ends of the line—Moscow and Vladivostok. To coordinate and oversee the work, the Trans-Siberia Committee was set up within the Russian government. By 1898, the builders had completed half of the single-line route.

The first passenger service on the line was instituted in 1899, with the

П3 0189

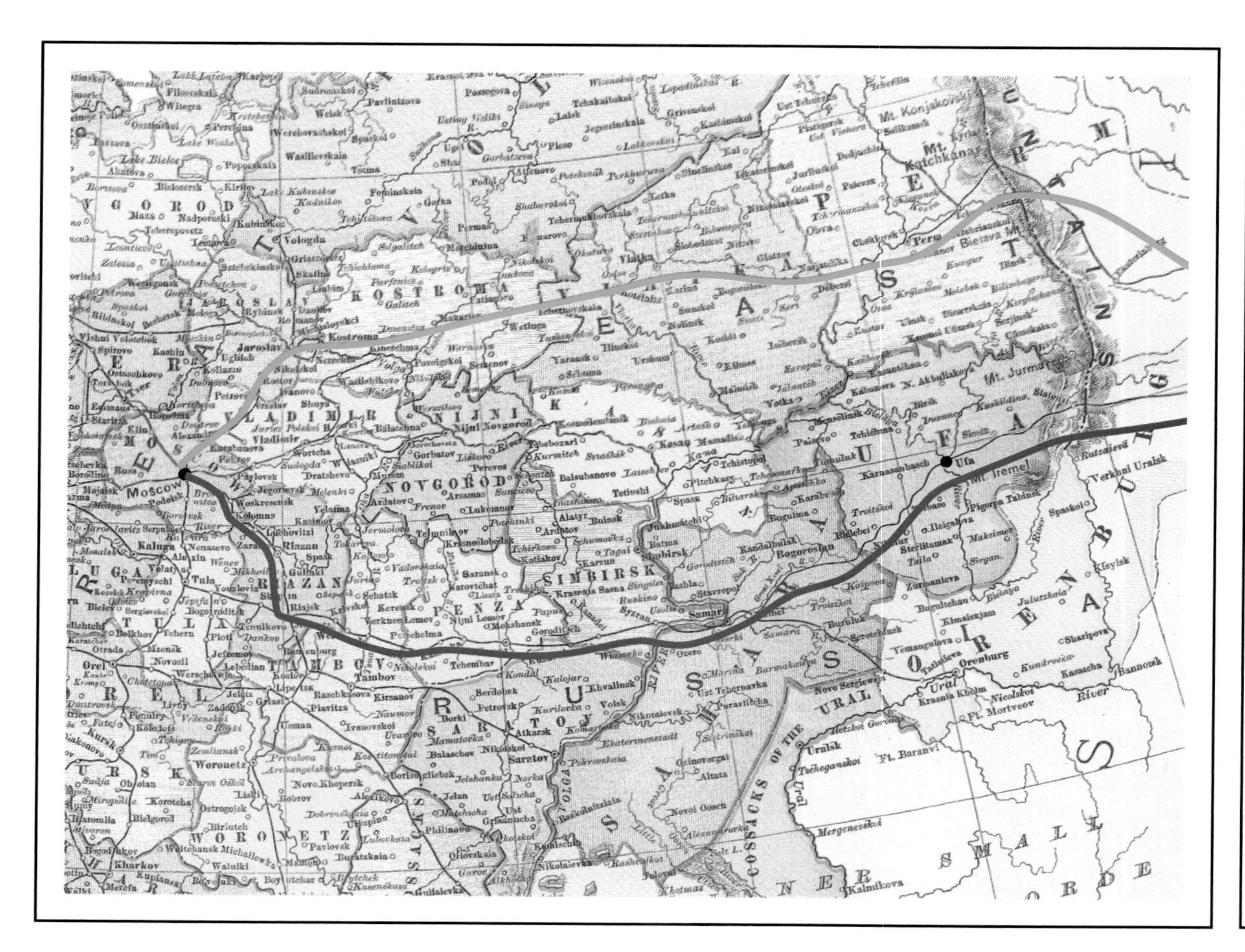

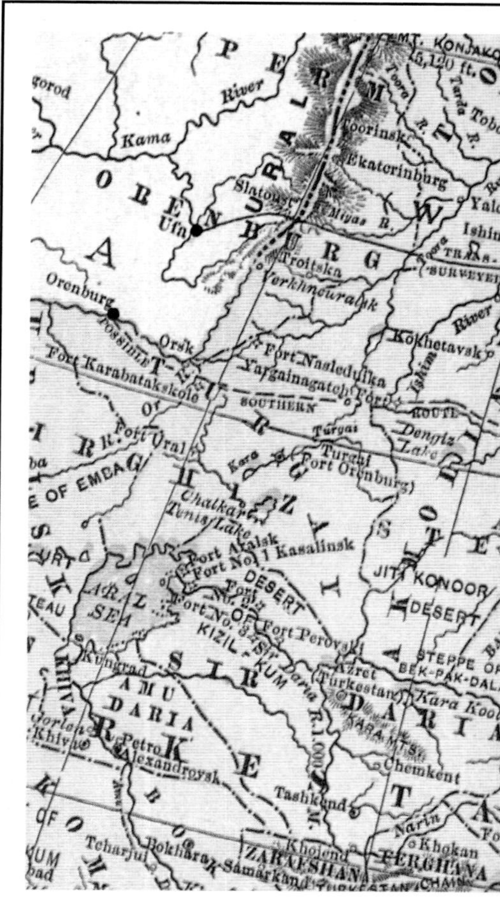

Siberia Express, which ran from Moscow to Tomsk, which is approximately 193 km (120 miles) east of Novosibirsk. The passenger cars on the *Siberia Express*, as well as its successor, the *Trans-Siberian Express*, were the products of an agreement between the Trans-Siberia Committee, headed by Czar Nicholas II, and George Nagelmackers, of Europe's Wagons-Lits Company. These were Pullman cars of opulent Wagons-Lits standard.

The *Siberia Express* timetable cited six days as the duration of the journey, but weather conditions could add days to that. The fact that it was as yet only a single line, and that the tracks were too light in construction, resulted in frequent breakdowns and derailings.

The planned main line ran fairly straight from Moscow to Taishet, approximately 1126 km (700 miles) east of Novosibirsk. At that point two routes were studied—one running by the northern edge of Lake Baikal, and one running by the southern edge of same.

The line east to the western edge of Lake Baikal was fairly level, following a fertile flatland that was bounded on the north by tundra and on the south by arid plains. At the lake, however, the mountains of the east began, and concomitant engineering difficulties arose.

As early as 1895, unfavorable engineering reports had cast a pall over plans to circumvent Chinese Manchuria by going north via mountainous Skovordino and Chabarovsk. Manchuria was comparatively flat, and was much easier going. Therefore, if the Chinese would agree to a line through Manchuria, the route past the southern tip of Lake Baikal was the way to go. The alternate, northern route would come into play years later, with some changes, as the Baikal-Amur Northern Main Line, which we will discuss later in this chapter.

A meeting was arranged with Chinese officials, and, luckily for the Russians, the Chinese chose as their envoy the Marquis Li Hung-chang, for he was a believer in railway construction (unlike many of his countrymen). The meeting resulted in the building of the Chinese Eastern Railway, which continued the Trans-Siberian Railway from Chita, approximately 643 km (400 miles) east of Lake Baikal, via

***Previous page:* The *Trans-Siberian* at Skovordino. *At right:* Nineteenth-century Moscow. *Above:* Trans-Siberian rail routes.**

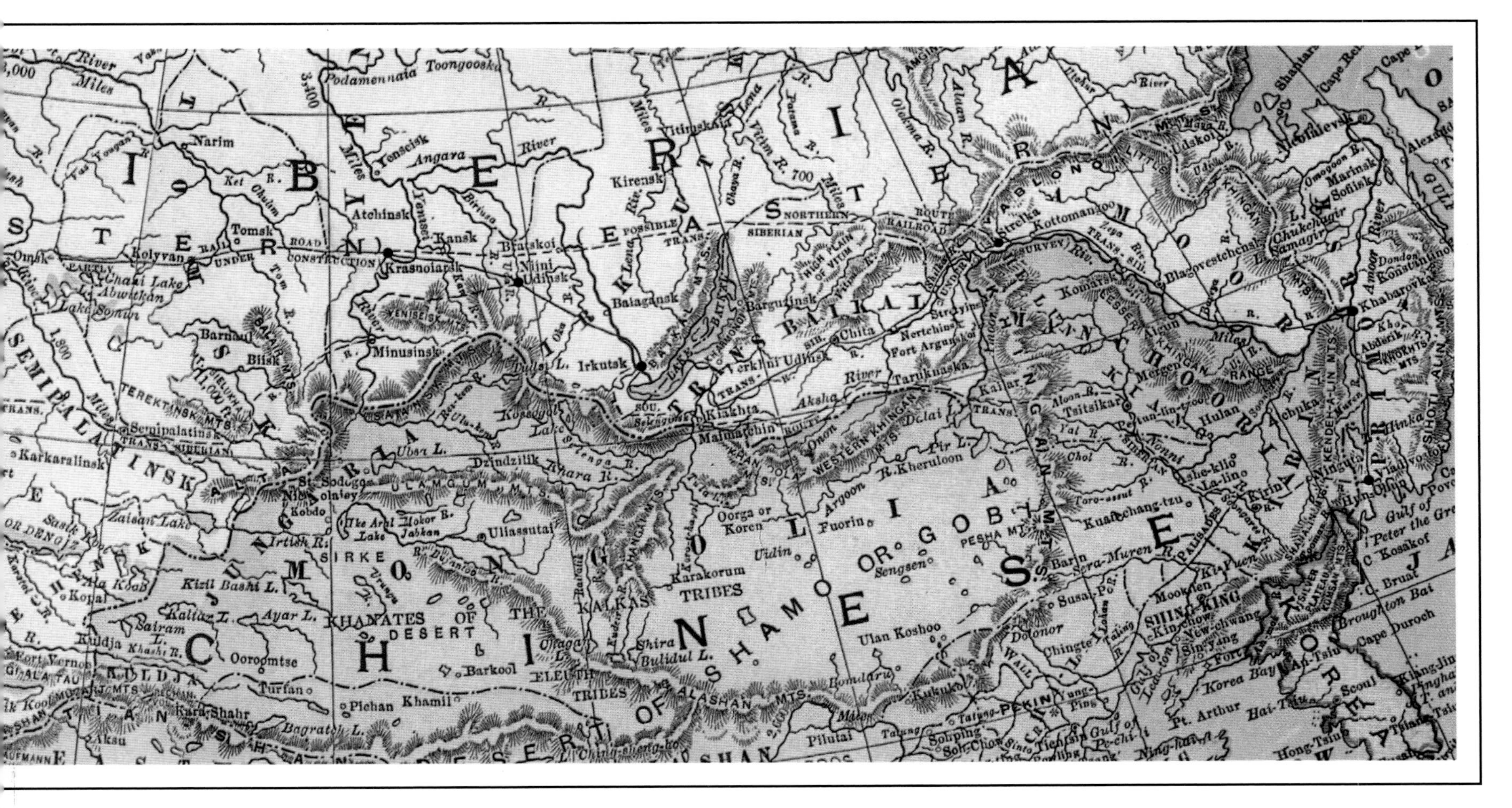

Harbin, in Manchuria, to Vladivostok, with a branch line directly south from Harbin to the Russian naval base in the Chinese port city of Port Arthur.

Given the difficult task at hand, the actual circumvention of Lake Baikal was seen as an unneccessary difficulty, and train ferry service was instituted to continue the line there in 1901. The train ferry proved unsatisfactory, and its shortcomings became apparent in early 1904, with the advent of the Russo-Japanese War. Men and supplies in the eastern reaches of Russia were in short supply, and Russia's only hope lay with the train.

The ferry was too vulnerable to weather changes. Lake Baikal, covered with winter ice, was therefore the site of an attempt to improve upon the train ferry. Rails were laid across the ice. Unfortunately, the first train to try the crossing broke through the ice and was lost.

This prompted progress on a line circumventing the lake on its southern shore. The Circum-Baikal Line, as it was called, was completed on 25 September 1904. Unfortunately, this was not enough to save the Russian cause, and in 1905, a peace treaty was signed between Russsia and Japan. Russia was forced to withdraw from Port Arthur, and gave the Japanese two-thirds of their share in the Chinese Eastern Railway.

The Trans-Siberia Committee then saw that it was necessary to circumvent the Chinese Eastern Railway, and construction on the more northerly Amur Line through Skovordino to Vladivostok was begun in 1908, and was completed in 1916—just in time to transport supplies from the US and a now-friendly Japan for Russia's losing effort in World War I.

Thus, the line was laid out and built in the fateful last years of Russian Czarist rule. It proved to be crucial to the revolutionary struggles between the Red and the White Russian armies during the turmoil of the Russian Revolution. With the Revolution and the assassination of the Czar and his family, and the dissolution of the Trans-Siberia Committee, all agreements were off with the Wagons-Lits Company. All 161 of the Wagons-Lits luxury cars were confiscated without any compensation to the company.

In fact, the continuance of the *Trans-Siberian Express* was a matter of some concern for those who had ridden the train before the Revolution, and had known the extraordinary completeness of its accommodations. In the first one-and-one-half decades of this century, *Trans-Siberian Express* trains carried a Wagons-Lits staff of 17, with one conductor doubling as a hairdresser, and another that was a qualified nurse, with a full dispensary at his disposal. In case of dire illness, a system was arranged whereby a telegraph message was sent to the train's next major destination, alerting an on-call doctor to meet the train when it pulled into the station.

The diner was open from 7:00 to 23:00, and the bathrooms were complete with hot and cold running water. Sleeper compartments were luxuriously appointed with velvet drapes and the finest bed linens. Stained glass and cut glass abounded in car partitions, and brass fittings, silver table service and linen table cloths adorned the diner.

Also, it was possible, by making connection with the Chinese Eastern Railway, to take a train from Moscow to Port Arthur or Peking, thus making the *Trans-Siberian Express* truly a train that traversed the Asian continent. Passengers could also travel from London to Shanghai via connections availed to the *Trans-Siberian Express* for approximately 70 British pounds—but it was an exceedingly long rail journey, as just the route from Moscow to Harbin (the connection south to China proper) consumed nine days' travel time.

However, the itinerary that lingers most in memory—as well as being the most used to this day—is the Moscow-Vladivostok line. It is the longest continuous railway in the world, at 9297 km (5777 miles). In keeping with the vast scope of the nation itself, the track width upon which the line was built by Imperial Russia was 1524 mm (five feet), making for a grand roominess in the cars used. This track gauge was later narrowed, albeit marginally, to 1520 mm (four feet, eleven inches) in 1972.

All in all, it was quite a journey—well over a week's duration. A traveler from Moscow to Vladivostok would have plenty of time to do whatever trainboard activity was available. A full library in four different languages was on hand, and chess and checker sets were also provided by the railroad. Perhaps some music? There was no ban on playing musical instruments, if the other passengers found it amenable.

What would the instrument be—guitar or balalaika? The train had an on-board piano, as well. One would have met a wide variety of Russian citizens, as well as Europeans, who loved to have the chance to explore this giant country that had long kept itself a mystery to the world.

On board the *Trans-Siberian Express*, one had the opportunity to meet Russian nobility, military officers, perhaps a few free-thinking intellectuals and landowners in the first class section; and soldiers (maybe some of the elite Cossacks), small merchants, a few recently-emancipated serfs en route to their chunks of land, an untamed artist, a free-thinker or two, Russian Orthodox pilgrims of all classes and backgrounds, and clerics of various rankings in the second-class section. This was pre-revolutionary 'Holy Russia,' dotted with monasteries and churches that were quite active.

After the Russian Revolution, the majority of churches, monasteries, clerics, Cossacks, free-thinkers, untamed artists, nobles and merchants big and small—and certainly all the landowners, be they nobles or serfs—disappeared, and most citizens of the newly-formed Union of Soviet Socialist Republics found themselves serfs in fact if not in title.

One manifestation of pre-revolutionary Russia that the materialist-minded Communists found absolutely necessary was the train route across Siberia—it was the only feasible way to transport material and personnel to the population-sparse expanses of far-eastern Russia.

When the Union of Soviet Socialist Republics was formalized on 30 December 1922, improvements to the Trans-Siberian Railway were resumed apace, with help from the

***At right:* A Soviet 2-6-2 steam locomotive. Steam still hauls the *Trans-Siberian Express* from Karimskoye to Belogorsk.**

СУ

United States and Japan. The Soviets have continued to upgrade the Trans-Siberian Railway over the years.

The *Trans-Siberian Express* continues to run, and requires seven days and two hours to cover the distance from Moscow to Vladivostok on the Circum-Baikal route of the Trans-Siberian Railway. One caveat to anyone seeking a rail journey in the Soviet Union: foreign nationals are allowed to board only those scheduled trains on which Intourist has an allocation of seats.

Soviet Railways classes their accommodations as either 'Soft,' with fully upholstered seats, or 'Hard,' with leather or plastic upholstery. These accommodations are carried through to the sleeping arrangements. Soft-class compartments are large and contain four large couchette berths per compartment. Hard-class sleeping provisions are of two kinds: bunks in four-berth compartments or open non-compartment coaches. Beds and bunks are convertible to seats for day use.

One has the choice of either Hard or Soft class accommodations on *Trans-Siberian Express* trains, with the addition that the *Trans-Siberian Express* offers conventional, European-style sleeping cars with two- and four-berth compartments.

Any library on the train could be expected to be heavily weighted with Communist tomes, and light reading might well be provided by such as Maxim Gorky, Andrei Vosnezhensky and, of course, Yevgheni Yevtushenko. There may be some Pushkin, the poet who is considered to be, even to this day, the writer of the 'soul of Russia,' and you may have some Chekhov, Gogol, Turgenev, Tolstoy, and maybe even some Mayakovsky (though he committed suicide while in disfavor with the Party). There may even be a

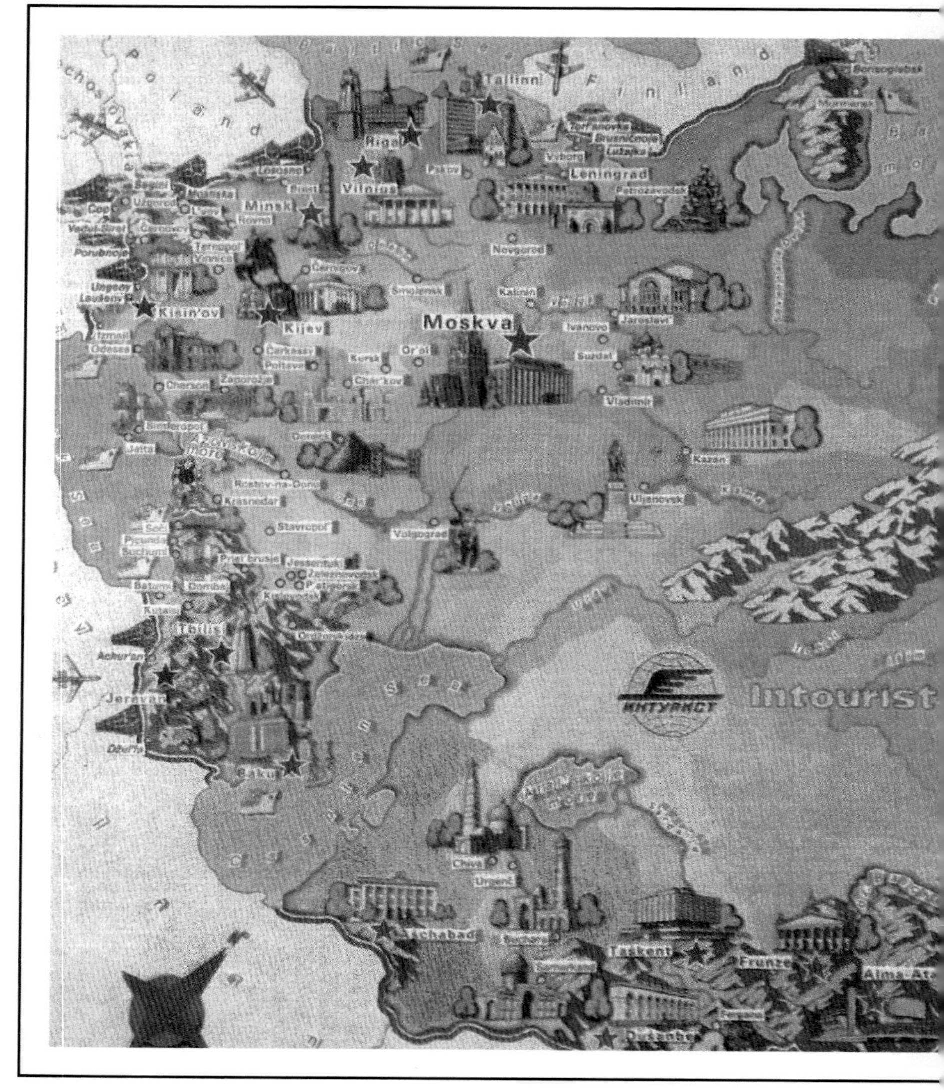

At right: **An Intourist map.** ***Above opposite:*** **A** ***Trans-Siberian Express*** **diner of 1900. The proposed salon** ***above*** **was never used.**

book or two by Dostoevsky (considered a genius but too religious) and Pasternak (a little too bourgeois), but probably nothing by the contemporary poets Josef Brodsky (an expatriate) and Irina Ratushinskaya (an expatriate), or the Nobel Prize-winning novelist Alexander Solzhenitsyn (though his books are being published in the USSR now).

On the train, you would meet a wide range of people from all over the vast USSR. Each would know precisely where they were headed, and each would have a certain reserve about both personal and political matters. With *perestroika*, there is some relaxation of the hyper-strict Communist yoke, yet there is still an appreciable atmosphere of tension.

By way of beverages aboard the *Trans-Siberian Express*, you'll have no problem obtaining black tea or vodka. One customary Russian way of drinking tea would make cavity-conscious Americans shudder: you hold a cube of sugar between your front teeth and drink the tea through it.

Food on board may well be another matter, as the USSR is famed for its shortages, so the cuisine may vary, especially as it is taken on as needed locally. World railway authority OS Nock is encouraging when he says that the quality of accommodations on the *Trans-Siberian Express* are on par with those established by Wagons-Lits at the beginning of the century (see above). The real uniqueness of this train route is its extraordinary expanse.

This is truly a train on which you can see a good bit of the world, and the time is coming when you will have a choice of routes on which to ride the *Trans-Siberian Express*. The originally abandoned plans for a more northern route have been modified and are being realized as the Baikal-Amur Northern Main Line. The Baikal-Amur Northern Main Line has not yet been used as an alternate to the Circum-Baikal Line as a regular route for the *Trans-Siberian Express*, as it is still under construction.

As for the traditional Circum-Baikal route, it has been

П36-0189

completely double-tracked. Much of it has been electrified, though as late as spring of 1990, steam locomotives could still be found pulling the *Trans-Siberian Express* on the non-electrified line east of Lake Baikal, from Karimskoye to Belogorsk. Diesels have apparently not been deemed romantic enough to head the fabled *Trans-Siberian Express*.

Any trip on the *Trans-Siberian Express* teaches passengers anew that the climate of the USSR varies from region to region, with Siberia evidencing great extremes—summers that are regularly in the high 20s and 30s of degrees Celsius (70s and 80s of degrees Fahrenheit), and winters that are sometimes tens of degrees colder than minus 31 degrees Celsius (minus 22 degrees Fahrenheit). This is the land of the fabled Russian steppes, endless tracts of grassy plain, and also of the Russian tundra, with its permafrost subsoil.

Lush forests, mountains, waterways and long stretches of flatland are also to be seen on this epic railway journey. Much of the trip from Moscow to Vladivostok takes place along the USSR's mammoth interior plain, broken notably by the Ural Mountains and the 3218-km (2000-mile)-long Volga River on its eastern half, and the Ob, Tangusta, Lena and Amur river systems, Lake Baikal and the Stanovoi Mountains on its western half.

The *Trans-Siberian Express* journey commences on a note of drama and history. The very heartbeat of Russia emanates from Moscow, which began as a twelfth-century walled fortress, or *kremlin*, built by a local prince. It is strategically located on the Moscow River, which is a tributary to the Oka, itself a tributary to that 'highway of Russian life,' the mighty Volga. In time, a village grew up around the fort, and Russian traders used the village's location to great advantage. The village, which took its name from the river, became a great trading center.

The area around the village and fort became the principality Muscovy. An event that gave the Prince of Moscow immense authority occurred in the fifteenth century, when the Byzantine Empire fell. The Byzantine princess Catherine fled to Moscow, where she wed Grand Duke Ivan III, 'the Great.'

With the marriage, the way was clear for the ordination of Ivan's successor to carry on the lineage of the Caesars that had passed on from ancient Rome to Constantinople, and from thence to Russia—hence, the Russian Czar, or Caesar. Ivan III established his sovereignity in the hearts of the disparate Russian peoples when he defeated a superior Mongol force, ending the Mongol domination of Russia, in 1480. In 1547, Ivan IV ascended the throne, and with a keen eye for defense, made fortress Moscow the seat of royal power.

The Cathedral of the Assumption was built within the 60-acre confines of the Kremlin. A Patriarch of the Russian Orthodox Church then located his Patriarchate at the cathedral, and Moscow became the spiritual center for the Christian peoples of the Russian land. Moscow thus occupies a place in the soul of each Russian as the traditional spiritual, as well as administrative, center.

Modern-day Moscow is a city of 8.6 million citizens. Along its bustling thoroughfares, Bauhaus-style block tenements and modern manufacturing facilities lie side-by-side with buildings and edifices that have existed for centuries. Among its famous landmarks are the Kremlin and the Church of St Basil—built in the sixteenth century at the behest of Ivan The Terrible. The concentric plan of the city echoes the brick and mud walls that once protected its inner environs from invaders.

At the other end of the Trans-Siberian Railway lies Vladivostok, the chief seaport of the USSR's Pacific coast. The city was founded in 1858, and began its strongest growth in 1905, when the port of Dalney fell to the Japanese in the Russo-Japanese War.

World War I strengthened Vladivostok's position as an important port, and in this century, the city has grown to a

At left: **A 4-8-4 steam locomotive with the westbound *Trans-Siberian Express* at Skovordino, the site of a historic convent.**

busy city of approximately 400,000 people. Inland from Vladivostok is Manchuria, and across the Sea of Japan is Japan's 'big island,' Honshu. On the way to Vladivostok, travellers will have a chance to stop in the important cities of Sverdlovsk, Omsk, Irkutsk, Skovordino and Khabarovsk.

If reading, music or chess playing is your *forte*, this is a rail journey during which you can at last read or play to your heart's content. The scenery is at times quite spectacular, but with the sheer length of travel, the above-suggested activities will get their share of attention.

In comparison to the Circum-Baikal Line, the still-unfinished Baikal-Amur Northern Main Line passes by the northern tip of Lake Baikal—via Bratsk, Chara, Tynda and Komsomolsk—before heading south to Vladivostok, or due east to the smaller seaport of Sovetskaya Gavan. Generally, this route runs from Tayshet, which is 563 km (350 miles) east of Irkutsk, to Khabarovsk, which is 643 km (400 miles) north of Vladivostok.

When completion of this line is accomplished, it will provide a rail link to the Soviet east that is 500 km (310 miles) shorter than the present Circum-Baikal Line routing of the Trans-Siberian Railway.

The Baikal-Amur Northern Main Line was begun in 1938. The far eastern section, from Komsomolsk to Urgal was opened on 2 July 1979, and the section from Kumora to Krasnoyarsk was opened in 1982. The line between Ust Kut and Tynda was completed in early 1984, and passenger service between Tynda and Moscow was then inaugurated.

The line from Tynda to Urgal was opened on 7 November 1984, and although through trains were running on that track at that time, it wasn't opened for regular Soviet Railways service until 1986. As of this writing, the line from Severobaikansk to Chara—between Kunerma and Tynda—is still in construction. A bit farther east, the line between Dinkiyy and Fevralsk is also under construction, and should some time soon be completed.

The class of service on the Baikal-Northern Main Line is as yet strictly of the 'Hard' class (see the discussion above). While through service from Moscow to Sovetskaya Gavan is yet delayed by construction, through service from Moscow to Severobaikansk, with diner-car accommodation, is currently running, but is limited to the summer period of July 1 to August 31. Other sections of the line in service are Sovetskaya to Nakhoda (due south on the line to Vladivostok), and Chegdomin, east of Severobaikansk, to Khabarovsk.

The western end of the Baikal-Northern Main Line crosses high mountain ranges for 750 km (466 miles): these include the Baikal, the North Mui, Udokan and Stanovoi mountains. Its complex geomorphology required that nine tunnels totalling 32 km (20 miles), 139 large bridges or viaducts and 3762 smaller bridges and culverts were built on the Baikal-Amur Northern Main Line.

At right: **An interwar-era 2-8-4 passenger engine.** ***Above:*** **The** ***Trans-Siberian*** **often carried pilgrims to monasteries like this.**

Transiberian Special and Peking Orient Express

Moscow — Peking	September 3-19, 1989	$5,590.00 — Double occupancy $6,620.00 — Single occupancy
Peking — Moscow	September 12-30, 1989	$5,590.00 — Double occupancy $6,620.00 — Single occupancy

Initial deposit: $500.00

For this spectacular journey we are using the best of Russian and Chinese deluxe coaches. This is the most unique way to combine a stay in Moscow, a most memorable trip through the beautiful Russian countryside, a visit to Peking and the Great Wall. Our rates include travel as described below, excursions, sightseeing tours and cultural programs during the voyage. Full board and accommodations throughout the journey in first class hotels with private bath/shower or in compartments aboard the train, all transfers (except airport transfers), and tour escort throughout the trip. Not included are airfares, visa costs and beverages.

MOSCOW — PEKING

Sept. 3	Arrive in Moscow on your own. Dinner and overnight at a first class hotel.
Sept. 4	Sightseeing and cultural performance in Moscow.
Sept. 5	Excursion to Zagorsk. After farewell dinner at the hotel you will board the Transiberian Special.
Sept. 6-7	Two days on board your own private deluxe train.
Sept. 8	Excursion to Novosibirsk and River Ob with folklore or theater performance.
Sept. 9	Full day on board the train.
Sept. 10	Sightseeing of Irkutsk with an afternoon circus performance. Overnight at the hotel.
Sept. 11	Excursion to Lake of Baikal, overnight at the Hotel.
Sept. 12-13	Board our deluxe train and spend two days traveling through magnificent countryside.
Sept. 14	Evening arrival at Ulan Bator, overnight at the hotel.
Sept. 15	After a sightseeing tour return to train for a farewell dinner on board.
Sept. 16	Arrive at the Mongolian border and during lunch time transfer to the Peking Orient Express. Welcome cocktail and dinner on board.
Sept. 17	Approx. 5 p.m. arrive in Peking. Transfer to our first class hotel.
Sept. 18	Excursion to the Great Wall and Ming tombs. Evening farewell and gala dinner, overnight at the hotel.
Sept. 19	Visit to the Forbidden City. Our program ends today but you might want to add a few more days in Peking or an extension to other places in the Orient.

PEKING — MOSCOW

Sept. 12	Arrive on your own in Peking. Dinner and overnight at our first class hotel.
Sept. 13	Visit of the Forbidden City.
Sept. 14	9 a.m. Departure by Peking Orient Express. Welcome cocktail and dinner on board.
Sept. 15	Full day visit to the Steam factory in Datong. Farewell dinner on board.
Sept. 16	Arrive at the Russian border. During lunch time we change to our Transiberian Special. Welcome cocktail and dinner on board.
Sept. 17	Morning arrival in Ulan Bator with sightseeing, overnight at our first class hotel.
Sept. 18	8 a.m. Depart Ulan Bator. Full day on board.
Sept. 19	Approx. 11 a.m. arrive at Lake Baikal. After lunch, sightseeing tour and hovercraft ride to Irkutsk. Dinner and overnight at the hotel.
Sept. 20	Sightseeing of Irkutsk. Evening departure by our private Transiberian Special.
Sept. 21	Full day on board.
Sept. 22-23	We are spending two days traveling along the famous BAM route via Severobaikansk.
Sept. 24	Today we enjoy a magnificent countryside traveling via Tayshet.
Sept. 25	After a full day on board we arrive in Novosibirsk. Overnight at the hotel.
Sept. 26	Full day sightseeing including River Ob. Approx. 9 p.m. depart by train for Moscow.
Sept. 27-28	Two full days on board our private train.
Sept. 29	Approx. 10 a.m. arrive in Moscow. Sightseeing tour including a cultural performance. Evening farewell dinner at the hotel.
Sept. 30	After breakfast at the hotel our tour ends but you might want to extend your stay for a few days in Moscow or travel to another destination.

Some of the largest bridges on the line are across the Lena, Zeya and Amur rivers, and are 500 meters (1640 feet), 1100 meters (3609 feet) and 1500 meters (4921 feet) in length, respectively. The longest tunnels include the Dusse-Alin, which is 1800 meters (1.1 miles) long; the Kodar, which is 2100 meters (1.3 miles) long; the Baikal, which is 6700 meters (4.2 miles) long; and the Severomuisky, which is 15,400 meters (9.6 miles) long.

It is a massive undertaking, for 1200 km (746 miles) of its trackage is in eastern Siberia—an area that is inhospitable to an extreme. Approximately nine months out of every year, snow falls to depths of two meters (6.9 feet), and most of the ground is permafrost to depths of five to 300 meters (916 to 984 feet). Winter temperatures are as low as minus 58 degrees Celsius (minus 67 degrees Fahrenheit)—yet, in the brief summer, temperatures can rise as high as 36 degrees Celsius (97 degrees Fahrenheit).

Even at the highest summer temperature, the permafrost thaws only as deep as one to 1.5 meters (three to five feet). Care must be taken during construction to preserve the extremely delicate ecological balance of this tundra region.

Tundra is notoriously unstable ground to build upon, being host to 'thermal karsts'—eroded limestone formations that collapse under loads; avalanche-prone scree slopes; and bogs. Many of the bridges and buildings in this area have to be supported on piles set as deep as 28 meters (94 feet). Eastern Siberia is also known for its earthquakes, sometimes as severe as eight or nine on the Richter scale. In the peak period from 1979–82, there were 4000 earthquakes in this area.

Most of the excavation and track-laying is, understandably, done by machines. The track lies on a bed of sand 200 mm (eight inches) and rock ballast 250 mm (10 inches) deep. However, the Soviets feel it's all worthwhile. In addition to shortening the Trans-Siberian Railway, the Amur-Northern Main Line promises to open up vast mineral resources.

An offshoot of this construction is in progress. This is a branch line from Berkatit, just above Tynda, to Yakutsk, deep in the northern Siberian interior. Just as the arteries of railroad steel reached into and opened up the frontiers of North America, so, too, are the continuing ramifications of the Trans-Siberian Railway aiding in the development of the Asian frontier.

Another kind of route extension was born directly from the *Trans-Siberian Express*. Through passenger trains from Moscow to Peking have been a regular offering by Soviet Railways in times past. This train service is called the *Far East*. There has been, however, a temporary suspension of this service, the reasons for which are not clear.

Briefly, the *Far East* has the same accommodations as the *Trans-Siberian Express*, and its journey is of eight days' duration. Proceeding along the Circum-Baikal Line to Vladivostok and Nakhodka, it then heads westward to Ulan Bator, then travels southeast to Peking.

In addition to the state-run *Trans-Siberian Express*, there is a specialty train, outfitted with fine, refurbished Russian and Chinese luxury coaches. This train is part of a 16-day extravaganza package that is offered by the Intraflug AG, the corporate force behind the *Nostalgie Istanbul Orient Express*.

The *Transiberian Special and Peking Express*, as the Intraflug service is known, follows the Circum-Baikal Line as far as Ulan Ude, then heads south to Peking via Ulan Bator. The *Transiberian Special and Peking Orient Express*, has amenities that are similar in nature to those enjoyed aboard Intraflug's *Venice-Simplon Orient Express* and *Nostalgie Istanbul Orient Express*, with more extensive involvement of hotels and extra-train tour activities. Please see the text chapter on those two trains.

Certainly, the *Trans-Siberian Express* is one way to get a relatively quick glimpse of the land whose myriad inhabitants call 'Mother Russia'—and perhaps you will find, first hand, the truth in what the Russian peasants used to say: 'Russia is not a country, it's a *world*.'

Japan's Shinkansen 'Bullet Trains'

urely, Japan has an undeniable allure for the inveterate traveller. That it is a nation equipped with some of the most-travelled rail trackage in the world, and that for just under two decades, the Japanese have excelled at providing express rail travel service, provides yet more attraction for the rail travel buff.

*Historically, Italy's **Il Settebello** is held to have ushered in the age of the modern, high-speed express train. Indeed, it seems that Europe in general has cornered the market on high-speed trains, with the recent advent of the French TGV (**Train à Grande Vitesse**) super express trains, which reach speeds of 270 kph (168 mph).*

*Be that as it may, there has long been the air of legend about the renowned super express trains of Japan. These are the famous **Shinkansen**, or 'Bullet Trains.' These are operated by the government-run Japan National Railways, which operates a number of other types of trains, as well.*

Japan National Railways moves approximately seven billion people

Toshiba
東芝
Toshiba
東芝
SUMMER DANCE
夏のおどり
NICHIGEKI
丸の内東宝劇
Music Hall

annually, and this transportation intensiveness is rendered even more remarkable by dint of the fact that only 15 percent of the nation's land area is flat enough to be fully developed for habitation and industry.

JNR operates as many as 28,000 trains daily. These trains are of six types. There are overnight sleeping car trains, or *Shindai-Ressha*; 'locals,' or *Futsu* trains; rapid trains or *Kaisoku*; express trains, or *Kyuko*; limited express trains or *Tokkyu*; and the famous super express, or *Shinkansen*, trains, with which we'll be dealing here.

But first, let's say that most JNR trains have 'deluxe' cars called 'green-sha' that require a surcharge on the basic fare; also, there is no smoking on short-distance trains, but long-distance trains have both smoking and nonsmoking cars. Luggage accommodations at stations tend toward very small lockers, and only at the largest stations are there rooms for storing one's luggage. There are also short-haul private lines to popular tourist attractions, but the Japan National Railways pass is not honored on these lines.

We will now focus on the famous *Shinkansen* (Japanese for 'new line'), known the world over as 'bullet trains' as much for their conical prows as for their high average speeds—161 kph (100 mph) on most lines, with top speeds of 209 kph (130 mph), and newer trains capable of 249 kph (155 mph), even though operational use of the increased speed capability has been delayed for some time.

The *Shinkansen* are distinctive, streamlined trains, with a striking white paint scheme having dark lateral stripes at wheel and window levels. This, combined with the bullet nose of the forward cab, creates an impression of a streaking projectile. Every axle is powered, and each car in the train is capable of 1000 horsepower.

Because of the high speeds sustained, *Shinkansen* trains run on a wider gauge track (1.4 meters or 4.7 feet) than that used by other Japanese trains, and are strictly passenger

Previous page: **A *Shinkansen* in Tokyo. *Above:* The Tokyo Station area. *Above opposite:* A *Tokkyu* lounge. *At right and above right:* *Shinkansens* in station. *Opposite:* On elevated track.**

carriers. Another difference between the *Shinkansen* trains and their contemporaries in Japan is the former's electrification at 25 kilovolts AC, instead of 1.5 kilovolts DC.

The Japanese have quite interesting technology to protect passengers from any possible untoward effects of traveling at high speed in tunnels, where their train is likely to be passed in the opposite direction by another *Shinkansen* train going at high speed.

At the entrance to a tunnel, sealing devices automatically go into operation. All vestibule and entrance doors are pressed so tightly closed that each compartment is almost hermetically sealed while the train is in the tunnel. The ride is, thanks to the sealing system and careful undercarriage engineering, very quiet and stable.

Seats are set up in a three-and-two pattern—therefore, each car has a passenger capacity of 110. On-train dining was limited to a buffet-style eating arrangement, but with the expansion of the New Tokaido Line from Tokyo-Osaka to Tokyo-Hakata—which necessitated a 19 km (11.5 miles) tunnel under the Kanmon Strait—full diner cars have been added to *Shinkansen* on that line.

Besides the buffet bar and diners, hostesses roam the train, carrying packed lunches (called *o bento*) for your convenience. Fish, eggs, vegetables, soybeans, pickles and rice are common fare for the boxed lunches, though an increasingly popular dish is eel in wine and soy sauce. Tea and milk round out a menu that is a bit fuller in the diner and at the buffet.

Traditionally, passengers obtained their *o bento* in the

JAPAN RAIL PASS

More convenience, lower cost for Japan sightseeing trips
Good on the entire Japan Railways Group network

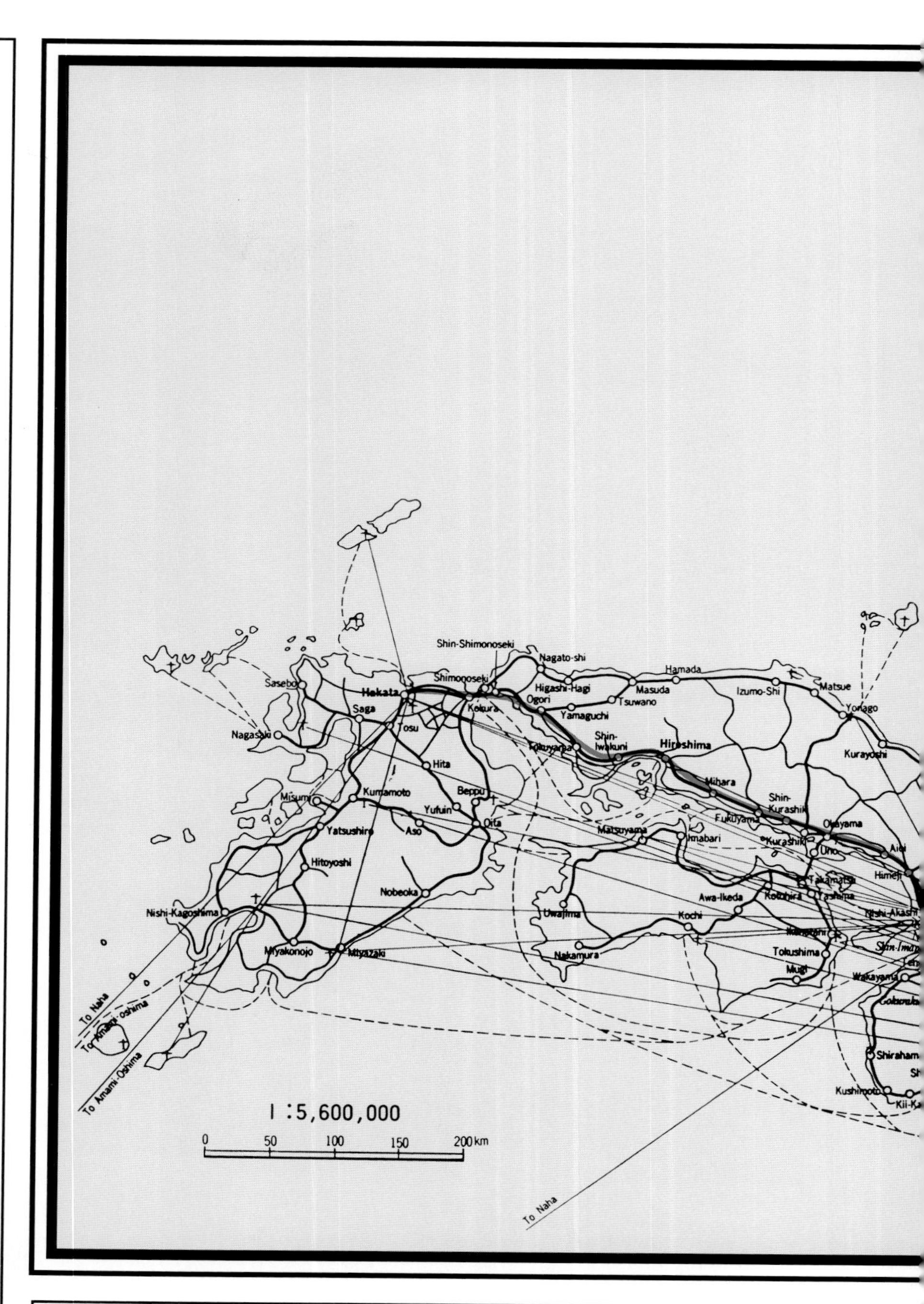

station, before boarding the train, and there were stations that took great pride in the quality of their *o bento*, as well as *o bento* boys who attained widespread notoriety for the quality of their service. The formalizing of this service on the trains is a welcome amenity.

The New Tokaido Line carries more than a half-million people on a single day, and while geographic obstacles restrain speeds in some areas to under 161 kph (100 mph), *Shinkansen* on that line still make the entire 664-mile journey in six hours and 56 minutes, for an average speed of 158 kph (98 mph).

Additionally, there is a *Shinkansen* line from Tokyo to Niigata, a port on the Sea of Japan; and from Tokyo to Morioka, a regional center on the northern end of Honshu. The Seikan Tunnel, connecting Honshu and Hokkaido under Tsugaru Strait, is, at 54 km (33.5 miles), the longest railway tunnel in the world. As of this writing, no *Shinkansen* line passes through this tunnel, but plans have been made to

***Above:* A Japan Rail Pass brochure, featuring a *Shinkansen* and Mount Fuji. *At right:* A view, from a *Shinkansen*, of Yokohama.**

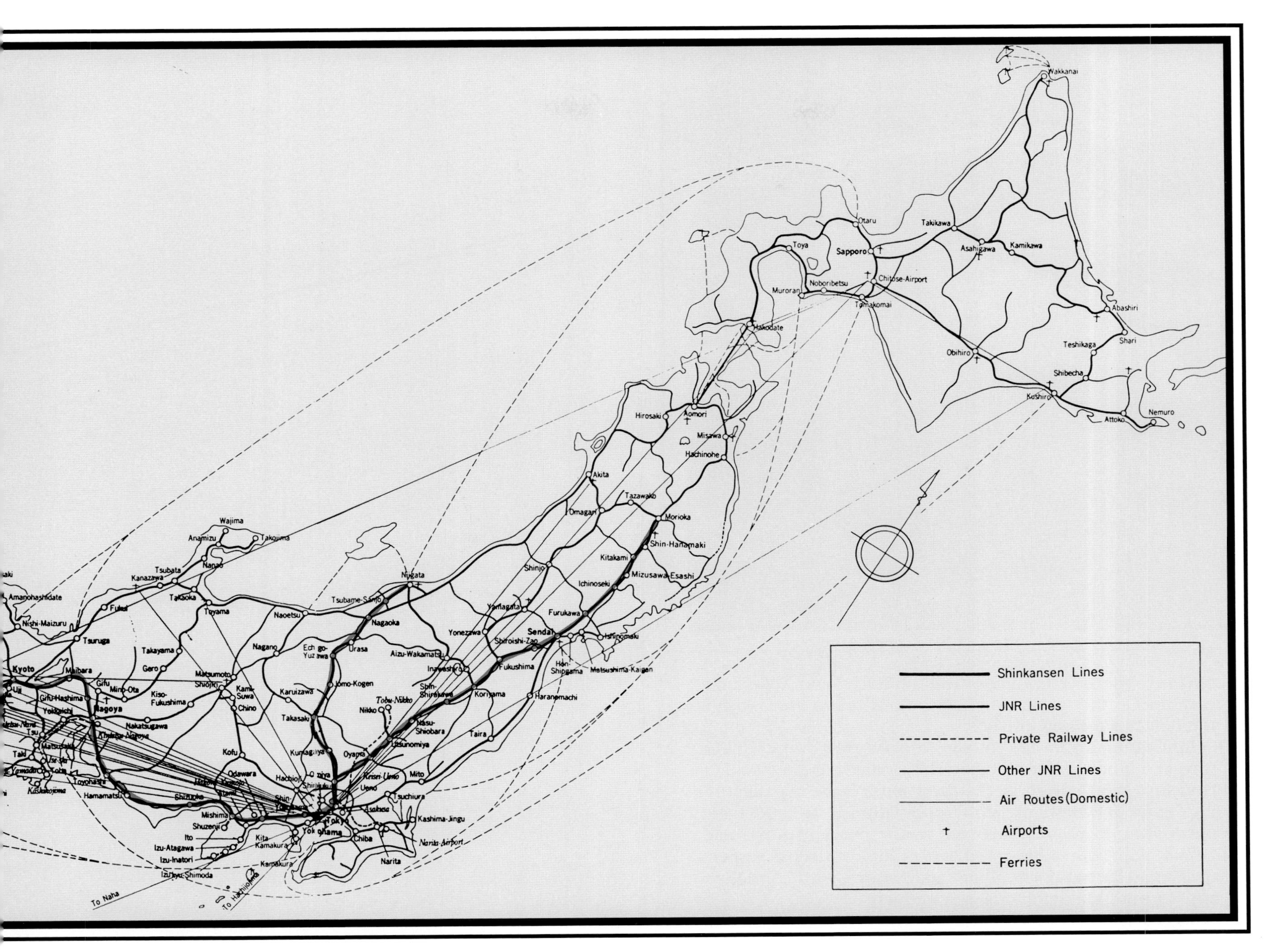

operate *Shinkansen* through it in the future. Currently, Japan National Railways' 'local' trains are operating through it.

Tokyo, the capital and largest city of Japan, has well over eight million citizens, and is a sprawling manufacturing and port city. It was, for centuries, a small fishing village called Yedo. Then, in 1603, the warrior Tokugawa chose it as his base of operations, setting up a shogunate that lasted until 1868. In 1869, the Emperor of Japan chose the town as the national capital, renaming it Tokyo, which means 'eastern capital,' as opposed to the old 'western capital,' which was Kyoto. The switch was made because Japan had begun a long trade association with the United States.

A mingling of old and new, with traditional Japanese architecture and Western-style buildings side by side, it is a city of contrasts. The almost totally modern business district is suffused with the Bauhaus-style buildings that so populate most contemporary urban centers. Many of the wealthier homes on its outskirts have Japanese gardens, with rippling ponds, bridges and dwarf pine trees. For many years, all distances in the nation were measured from the Nihon-Bashi ('Bridge of Japan') that crossed the Sumida River in the financial district.

Now a world-class port city, its famous Cherry Blossom Festival draws millions of visitors every year. One would not suspect that, in its history, Tokyo suffered a catastrophic earthquake in 1923, was almost completely destroyed by American bombs in World War II, and suffers typhoons every autumn. Yet it continues as the very heart of Japan.

Just a few miles southeast of Tokyo lies the major manufacturing and port city of Yokohama, with three million

citizens. The metropolitan areas of Tokyo and Yokohama combine in the world's most populous urban area, with a total of 25.4 million citizens.

Emanating from Tokyo, the *Shinkansen* routes make travel to other major cities on the Japanese main island of Honshu a swift enterprise. Farthest south is the manufacturing center of Hiroshima, with a population of 910,000; lying north from Hiroshima are the major ports of Kobe and Osaka, with 1.3 million and 2.6 million citizens, respectively; and farther north, Kyoto and Nagoya, with 1.4 million and 2.1 million inhabitants, respectively.

Tokyo itself is surrounded by the largest lowland in Japan—the Kwanto, or Tokyo, Plain, and a consequent concentration of population. To the north is the manufacturing center of Sendai, with 600,000 population. Also, smaller but important cities lie across the island, toward the Asian mainland—the port city of Niigata; and at the southernmost tip of the *Shinkansen* line to the island of Kyushu—the city of Hakata.

This latter *Shinkansen* line must traverse the mountainous spine of the island of Honshu, but it is one of the most scenic, with views of the country's upland evergreen forests. The north-south *Shinkansen* routes must traverse the populous shoreline corridor, and in order to facilitate speedy running, grade crossings are avoided by the simple expedient of using elevated track beds.

Environmentalists have, in the past decade, complained vehemently about the trains' environmental impact, citing noise as a predominant problem. However, as we have said, the noise level inside the trains is extraordinarily low, and the ride is confidence-inspiring. Perhaps Japan National Railways will find a way to reduce the exterior noise level of their *Shinkansen* as well.

Some visitors to Japan may be more interested in the *Shindai-Ressha* sleeping car trains, which are said to be on a standard with such great trains as Australia's *Indian-Pacific*. However, if you're going to go 'first cabin' in Japan, the way to go is by the *Shinkansen* 'bullet trains.' For a nation that has always been driven to maximizing its land area, the *Shinkansen* represents a high point of Japanese industry and time-economy.

***Above: Shinkansens* of the New Tokaido Line in station. *At right:* Tokyo Central Station, the major rail hub of Japan.**

TAXI
無線タクシー
のりば

The Blue Train of South Africa

*one, or at least few, doubt that the **Blue Train** is the most luxurious train in the world, with on-board suites of rooms a hallmark. This luxurious train has been operated since 1946, and if you take into account its predecessor, then luxury service on the Cape Town-Pretoria route has been continuous (with an exception for World War II) since 1903.*

This route was an extension of South Africa's first transcontinental railway, built to connect the diamond mines and the gold mines of the interior with the coastal cities of Cape Horn and Durban. The transcontinental line was completed on 10 October 1895, and it ran from Cape Town to Durban by way of Heidelburg, just south of Johannesburg. A feeder line was run to the gold-processing center of Johannesburg, continuing northward to Pretoria.

The South African topography is quite rugged, and the line climbs from near sea level at Cape Town to 1748 meters (5735 feet) in altitude at Johannesburg, with some gradients as steep as one in 40. The line's builders deemed it wise to construct the whole of it in narrow gauge

3126

track, which is 1067 mm (three feet, six inches) wide, to better negotiate construction through this often mountainous terrain.

The importance of passenger travel was addressed in 1903, with the inauguration of an elaborate passenger train with sleeper cars, which ran from Cape Town to Pretoria. The rolling stock of this train was matched to the finely crafted cabins aboard the Union Castle mail-and-passenger steamships arriving at Cape Town from England. After all, many of the steamship passengers would make connection with the train for transportation to points in the South African interior.

When the Union of South Africa was formed in 1910, the independent railways that had operated sections of the transcontinental line merged, to become South African Railways. As a consequence, the luxury train was named the *Union Limited*. This was an all-first-class express, and was on a level with such grand European express trains as the *Orient Express*.

The *Union Limited* ran two days per week, with an ultimate elapsed time from Cape Town to Johannesburg of 29.75 hours. There was also a train for passengers of all classes that ran the route five days per week. This train reached Johannesburg in 39 hours, considerably slower than the *Union Limited*.

Previous page: **Steam saw use on the *Blue Train* route *(above opposite)* until 1977. *At right:* A *Blue Train* suite. *Above:* A lounge. *Opposite:* Narrow track gauge for a rugged terrain.**

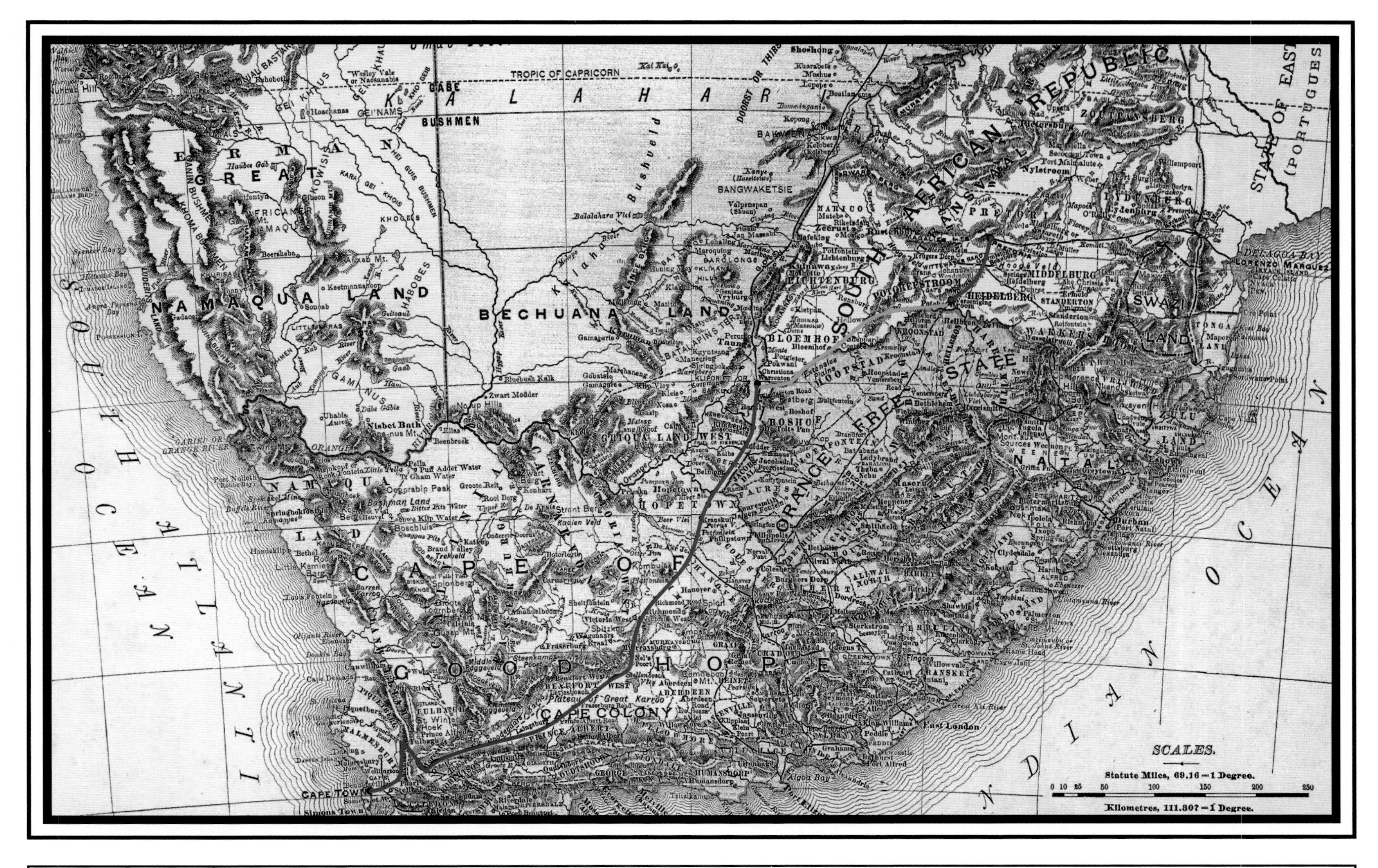
TROPIC OF CAPRICORN
BUSHMEN
BECHUANA LAND
NAMAQUA LAND
SOUTH AFRICAN REPUBLIC
ORANGE FREE STATE
CAPE OF GOOD HOPE
CAPE COLONY
NATAL
CAPE TOWN
SOUTH ATLANTIC OCEAN
INDIAN OCEAN
DELAGOA BAY
East London
Durban
SCALES.

The *Union Limited* became increasingly popular over the years, necessitating more cars in its makeup, which in turn required heavier locomotive power. Among the first locomotives used by the *Union Limited* were 4-6-2 Pacific-type passenger locomotives, but these were replaced by giant 4-8-2 Mountain-type locomotives in the 1930s.

By this time, the *Union Limited* was equipped with a diner car that included a bar, large sleeping compartments with private shower facilities and an observation car at the rear of the train. With such luxurious amenities, a first-rate staff was necessary to make the luxury train truly complete, and the *Union Limited* had staffing that was second to none, including valet service.

As a consequence of the narrow gauge, the South Africans developed car design over the years to allow for a greater *loading gauge* than might be imagined. For years, South African rail cars and locomotives have had a maximum height of four meters (13 feet, seven inches), and a maximum width of three meters (10 feet), which is larger than the rolling stock on some standard gauge, 1435 mm (four feet, eight inches) rail lines.

In the late 1930s, plans were made for an ultra-luxurious train to replace the aging *Union Limited*. This train was to be of a high level of luxury, indeed. In 1937, South African Railways contacted the British car-building firm of Metropolitan-Cammell, and an order was placed for fully air-conditioned all-steel cars, built in matched sets for each train running the schedule.

The cars were painted a distinctive blue, with a white stripe along their upper sides. Steam was then the main motive power on South African trains, and, in contradistinction to the modern *Blue Train*'s matching blue electric and diesel locomotives, this original *Blue Train*'s locomotives were painted black, as were all of South African Railway's steam locomotives.

The cars were delivered in 1939, and though the train is held to have originated in 1939, its legendary appellation was not officially bestowed until later. World War II interrupted all plans for a gala inauguration. However, the new train sets did service until 1942, whereupon the exigencies of the war dictated that they be put in storage until peacetime.

In 1946, the cars were rolled out of storage for a debut under the now-famous name of the *Blue Train*. This train featured an Art Deco-tinged modernism in its interior

At right: **The *Blue Train* with electric power.** ***Above right:*** **On the *Union Limited*.** ***Above and opposite:*** **Vintage steam for grades.**

appointments. Accommodations on board included private showers in strictly private sleeping compartments of a variety of arrangements, the top of the line being a multi-room suite for two.

This was complemented by an opulent diner and an observation car on the rear of the train, plus a lounge with a stand-up bar, tables and stuffed chairs and a sofa. This lounge had plenty of atmosphere, due to its oblique lighting and a feeling of openness imparted by its tastefully arched ceiling.

However, as it had in 1937, South African Railways once again got the urge for something even grander. This was to be a second-generation *Blue Train*. The cars for this train were made in South Africa by Union Carriage & Wagon, and were designed to be extraordinarily luxuriant, with styling that is squarely in the Modern school. This new *Blue Train* was inaugurated on 4 September 1972.

At that time, all the route save that stretch between Beaufort West and Kimberley was electrified, and distinctively-painted blue electric locomotives powered the *Blue Train* on those parts of the line. However, the old black-painted steam locomotives still hauled the train for the non-electrified part of the route, and this was deemed unacceptably anachronistic for the brand-new *Blue Train*. Therefore, the steam locomotives were replaced by diesels that wore the *Blue Train*'s blue-with-yellow-stripes locomotive colors.

The *Blue Train*'s former cars were assigned to South Africa's other luxury train line, the Durban-Johannesburg *Drakensburg*, which in another incarnation was the *Trans-Natal*. This train's colors are South African Railways russet with a burnt orange chevron on the locomotive.

The *Blue Train* currently carries 108 passengers in 16 coaches. Its amenities are of such stature that it is ranked as a five-star hotel. Normally, a narrow-gauge railway produces pronounced sway and unevenness of ride, but the *Blue Train*'s cars are specially designed for an even, smooth ride, with air-cushioned bogey trucks instead of the old-fashioned spring-cushioned trucks.

All sleeping accommodations are in private rooms, and dinner demands semi-formal to formal attire. A staff of 26

Above opposite: **One of the 4-6-2 Pacific locomotives that were 'flatlands' transport for the *Union Limited*, and parts of the *Blue Train* route. *Above:* In the elegant *Blue Train* diner.**

BLUE TRAIN
BLOUTREIN
SOUTH AFRICAN
TRANSPORT SERVICES
CATERING DEPARTMENT
SUID-AFRIKAANSE
VERVOERDIENSTE
VERVERSINGSDEPARTEMENT

MENU • SPYSKAART

BREAKFAST/ONTBYT

Chilled orange juice
Verkoelde lemoensap

Stewed fruit
Gestoofde vrugte

Sorghum porridge and fresh milk
Sorghumpap en vars melk

Corn flakes and fresh milk
Mielievlokkies en vars melk

Poached fish with cheese sauce
Geposjeerde vis met kaassous

Hamburger steak with mushrooms
Hamburgvleis met sampioene

Pork sausage with mashed potatoes
Varkwors met kapokaartappels

Broiled bacon
Geroosterde spekvleis

Eggs to order
Eiers volgens bestelling

Tea / Tee — Toast / Roosterbrood — Coffee / Koffie

Marmalade / Marmelade — Jam / Konfyt — Honey / Heuning

Dining Car Manager
Eetwabestuurder
H.H. Weirauch

Head Chef
Hoofsjef
D.A. Botha

1988-09-06
T5*

BLUE TRAIN
BLOUTREIN
SOUTH AFRICAN
TRANSPORT SERVICES
CATERING DEPARTMENT
SUID-AFRIKAANSE
VERVOERDIENSTE
VERVERSINGSDEPARTEMENT

MENU • SPYSKAART

LUNCHEON/MIDDAGETE

Stuffed tomato
Gevulde tamatie

Thick vegetable soup paysanne
Dik groentesop paysanne

Sole with white-wine sauce
Tongvis met witwynsous

Crayfish mayonnaise
Kreefmayonnaise

Tournedos with parsley butter
maitre d'hôtel
Tournedos met pietersieliebotter
maitre d'hôtel

Roast loin of pork with apple sauce
Gebraaide varklende met appelsous

Assorted vegetables
Verskeidenheid groentes

Cold meats and salads
Koue vleis en slaai

Coffee mousse
Koffiemousse

Ice-cream with caramel sauce
Roomys met karamelsous

Cheese and biscuits
Kaas en beskuitjies

Coffee
Koffie

Dessert

Dining Car Manager
Eetwabestuurder
H.H. Weirauch

Head Chef
Hoofsjef
D.A. Botha

1988-09-05

T5*

attends to the passengers. Just as in a traditional hotel, guests' shoes left in a locker by their compartment door at night are given a glossy shine by a staff member employed to do this. A push of a button in a passenger's compartment will call a steward to provide snacks or drinks from the diner or the lounge bar.

Those who desire the utmost in privacy can, for a surcharge, have all meals brought to their rooms. Also, the amount of natural light flooding a compartment is regulated by venetian blinds, set between the tinted panes of glass that form the outside windows. These blinds are operated by means of a knob that is located on the compartment's control panel, which also features the room service call button and the air conditioning temperature control (adjustable by the passenger).

Each compartment also has a push-button radio with three channels: Radio South Africa, the national broadcast; Springbok, which is the commercial channel; and a taped music program. Also, South African Railways provides a guidebook to the train's facilities and some of the highlights on the route. This really is more a book than a pamphlet, and is clearly symbolic of the level of luxury and opulence that is attained by the *Blue Train*. With 40 pages in full color, a cloth cover and spiral binding, this is no mere gatefold broadside.

There is little traffic in the corridors of the *Blue Train*, and those who stray from their compartments are either going to the diner, or are headed for the incomparable lounge car. A bar with fashionable stools is located at one end of the lounge car, and the remainder of the lounge features comfortable chairs and nicely-designed tables, plus bouquets of tastefully arranged flowers here and there. Recessed ceiling lights give off a warm and mellow glow. The bar features snacks and a full range of the finest drinks. Sleeping accommodations are, as we have said, strictly private compartments. Also, the *Blue Train* departs from the rather inconvenient norm of South African Railways trains in that sheets, pillowslips and blankets are provided at no extra cost.

The most luxurious sleeping accommodation is a three-room suite for two passengers. The bedroom of this suite features non-convertible twin beds, with a bedside table and reading lamps built into the headboard, plus a dressing table with mirrors and a wardrobe closet. Adjoining this is a

private lounge with beverage refrigerator and a cabinet for drinking glasses, plus two armchairs and a settee.

Just off the private lounge is a full-scale bathroom, complete with a large bathtub, and a wardrobe closet. This suite occupies one car with two other sleeping accommodations, each with its own private fully-equipped bathroom: a convertible bedroom/dayroom with space for three people and its own private bathroom; and the other is a single-occupancy compartment.

The next level of accommodation has three rooms per railcar. One of these is for single occupancy, while the other two are for two to three people. Each has its own private shower and toilet facilities. Ample floor space in the two-to-three person rooms allows room for a table and two armchairs, plus the bench seat into which a lower berth converts.

Also, there are lower-priced accommodations that are less roomy and make use of a common shower at the end of the car in which they are housed. Every compartment has hot and cold water on tap in its washbasin, as well as a third faucet that dispenses ice-cold drinking water.

The dining car has tables laden with silver utensils and serving ware of every description, napkins and tablecloths of a satiny ecru, silver bowls overflowing with fresh fruit on the polished wood sideboard, and fresh bouquets of flowers everywhere. All this is lit by inobtrusive light that glows softly on the fine wood panelling.

No matter what your level within this strictly first-class service is, however, there is no surcharge for the gourmet meals in the diner—alcoholic beverages are the only items subject to such charge. The full breakfast menu offers coffee and juice; a choice of poached haddock or sautéed kidneys;

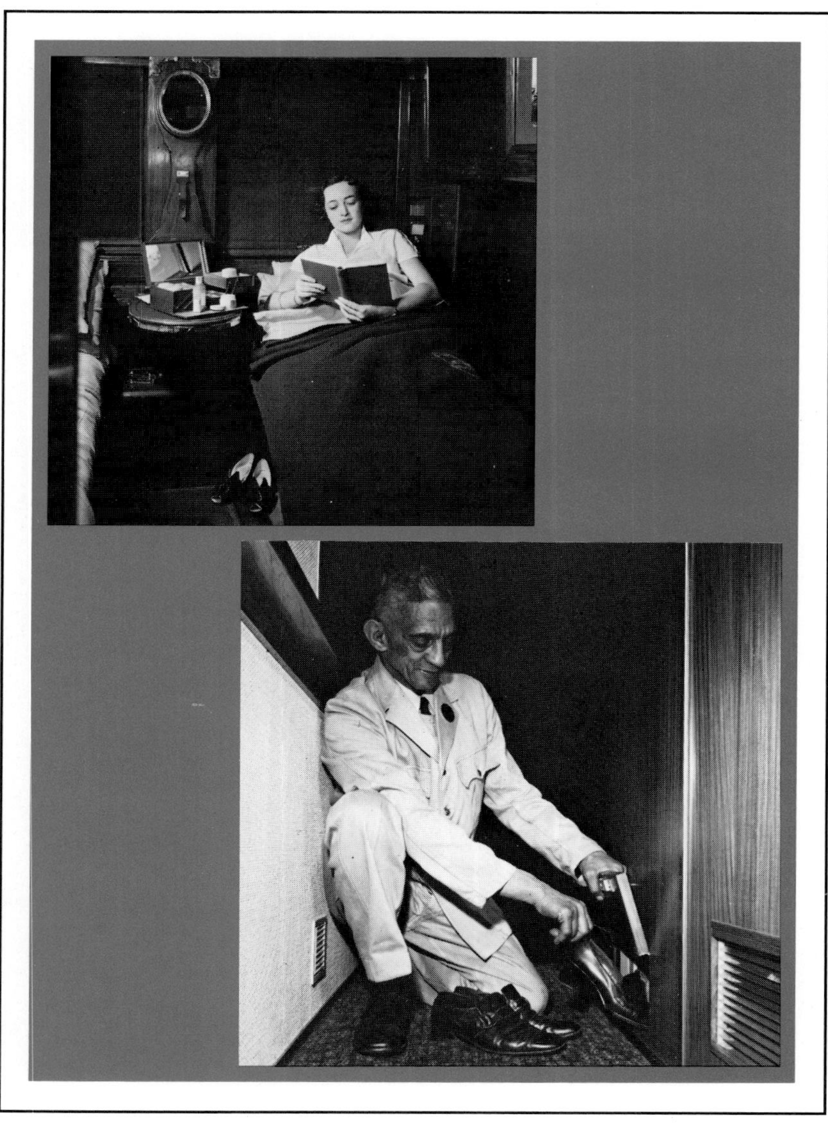

Previous pages: **The *Blue Train*. *Above:* A late steam locomotive. *Opposite, above and below:* Second- and third-grade rooms. *At right:* Valet service. *Above right:* On the *Union Limited*.**

or bacon, sausages and eggs cooked in any style desired.

Lunch typically begins with a fruit cocktail, and may move on to lobster. The next offerings include a choice of fillet of beef or leg of lamb, and the meal is finished with pudding, cheese, fresh fruit and coffee. Dinner offerings include appetizers, main dishes, side dishes and desserts such as fruit cocktail, cream soup, fried sole with *sauce tartare*, lamb cutlet with *sauce reforme*, roast stuffed turkey, beef sirloin, asparagus with mayonnaise, spring vegetables, Bavarian chocolate cream pudding, pear melba, cheese, fresh fruit and coffee. The wine list offers a delectable variety of wines.

The *Blue Train* also has car ferry service, whereby passengers can bring their private vehicles with them for use at their destination. The *Blue Train* covers the 1609 km (994 miles) from Pretoria to Cape Town in 25 hours and 20 minutes, and returns in 25 hours and 32 minutes.

The *Blue Train* makes its run on Mondays from January to October 10, and on Mondays, Wednesdays and Fridays from October 11 to the end of December, taking advantage of the seasonal weather change. Reservations are obligatory, and can be made up to 11 months in advance for accommodation aboard the *Blue Train*.

The landscape along the route is a combination of verdure and rock outcroppings, with level stretches broken by what seem at times to be precipitous climbs and descents. Further accents are added to this journey by the Vaal and Orange rivers, and by sightings of South African wildlife.

Going from Pretoria to Cape Town, the *Blue Train* sets out from Pretoria at 10:00 on the first day of travel. Pretoria is the capital of the Republic of South Africa, as well as of its home province, Transvaal. With 303,684 citizens, it is a bustling administrative center, and is the site of the Voortrekker Monument to the Dutch pioneers who first colonized the high veldt.

The train strikes out across the grasslands to Johannesburg, the first stop on the itinerary. Though the *Blue Train* stops a mere 20 minutes here, this city of 642,232 inhabitants is crucially important to the nation's economy. It is a processing center for the gold ore-rich Witwatersrand (in translation, 'White Waters Ridge'), or, coloquially, the 'Rand.' The surface deposits of the Rand were long ago mined out, so the South Africans have dug the world's deepest gold mines, over 3353 meters (11,000 feet) deep.

More grasslands terrain rolls past the windows en route to another interesting stop on the route: Kimberley, at 18:46. This city of 105,258 people is famous for its diamond fields, which were discovered in 1869, and were a major factor in South Africa's long-time dominance of the world diamond supply market.

The *Blue Train* departs Kimberley at 19:06. With evening coming on, the lounge or the diner may be the preferred place on the train for most passengers. None of the stops on the *Blue Train*'s route are for more than 20 minutes, and touring will be a matter of reprising the route on lesser trains, and taking local transit, which includes local trains and buses.

The stops through the night are De Aar, at 22:11 and Beaufort West, at 2:09. The first town of any size passengers see in the morning is Worcester, at 8:32 on the second day. The *Blue Train* pauses here for a mere two minutes, before plunging on down the coastal hills toward Cape Town, arriving there at 11:20. This bustling port was crucial to the development of South Africa, and is a history buff's delight.

Tourists seeking more economical travel than the *Blue Train* may be interested in the *Trans-Oranje*, which makes a journey from Durban, via Kroonstad and Bloemfontein, to Cape Town, circumventing Johnannesburg and Pretoria, in approximately 35 hours. The *Trans-Oranje* features accommodations that range from first to third class. Even so, few can resist the opportunity for a rail journey aboard the fabulous *Blue Train*.

At right: **A lounge aboard the *Blue Train*. The *Blue Train* is considered to be the most luxurious rail service in the world.**

ART GALLERY & GARDENS, CAPE TOWN.

These pages: **Cape Town, as it was when steamer traffic from Europe necessitated the building of the South African transcontinental railway line.**

Canada's VIA Rail Canadian

*ia Rail's **Canadian** is the proud heir of a long tradition of North American **trains deluxe**, and is one of the comprehensive rail travel offerings of Canada's nationalized passenger system. VIA Rail offers train routes to nearly any civilized part of the vast nation of Canada. Among the other excellent trains that travel these routes are the **Atlantic**, the **Ocean**, the **Chaleur**, the **Skeena** and the new LRC ('Light, Rapid and Comfortable') trains. Of these, the **Canadian** has long been the very epitome of excellence in Canadian rail service.*

The LRC trains feature reclining seats, panoramic windows, baggage stowage, reading lights, restrooms, snack and meal service and cellular phone service. These trains are capable of speeds up to 152 kph (94 mph), and traverse the Quebec City–Windsor inter-city corridor, making stops at Montreal, Ottawa, Kingston, Toronto and London.

*However, the most renowned of VIA Rail's trains are called 'transcontinentals,' among which is the **Canadian**. Generally, these have sleeping accommodations and dining facilities, and make connections*

6306

with regional rail diesel car trains for those who wish to tour an area thoroughly. The *Atlantic* goes from Quebec through Maine to New Brunswick and Nova Scotia via Montreal, Sherbrook, Saint John, Moncton, Truro and Halifax. The *Ocean* follows the St Lawrence River from Montreal to Moncton. The *Chaleur* wends its way through the Gaspé region of Quebec, stopping at Carleton, New Carlisle, Percé and Gaspé.

Transcontinental trains that tour the western Canadian landscape also make connections with train service from Winnipeg to Churchill, Manitoba, on Hudson's Bay. Yet further ramifications of the Canadian railway system allow exploration of this fabulously scenic country by way of such historic destinations as Moosonee, at the southern tip of Hudson Bay, and Fort McMurray in northern central Alberta.

The *Canadian* is the most prestigious of the VIA Rail transcontinentals, making a journey of 4467 km (2776 miles) through some of the most scenic and awe-inspiring landscape that Canada has to offer—part of the reason that the *Canadian* has long been the pride of the Canadian railways.

It was originally operated by Canadian Pacific Railways, in the days before Canadian Pacific and its long-time competitor, Canadian National, had their passenger service consolidated in the present-day VIA Rail system. Upon its inauguration on 24 April 1955, the *Canadian* faced direct competition from the CN's *Super Continental*, which was inaugurated that same day. Both trains offered excellent dining facilities, plush sleepers, observation cars and a full range of passenger amenities.

However, the sleek *Canadian*, with its shining aluminum Scenic Dome cars, triumphed over the *Super Continental*, with its twin green-and-gold diesel locomotives. The *Canadian* at that time offered the longest dome car train ride in the world, running from Montreal to Vancouver over a distance of 4675 km (2905 miles).

This route has been modified several times, the first major change being in October 1978, when the *Canadian* commenced running only from Toronto to Vancouver, following

Previous page: The _Canadian_. _Above:_ A transcontinental railway workers' camp at Lake Superior. _At right:_ A construction train—and snow shed construction _(above opposite)_—in the Rockies.

the old Canadian Pacific cross-country line via Sudbury, Winnipeg, Medicine Hat, Calgary and Banff.

The routing of the *Canadian* was changed again on 15 January 1990. As of that date, the train follows a more northern route, along the old Canadian National line, from Toronto to Vancouver via Winnipeg, Saskatoon, Edmonton and Jasper.

The *Canadian*'s success is only to be expected. This train has a pedigree that goes back to the creation of the first Canadian transcontinental line, the Canadian Pacific Railway. When the United States completed its epochal transcontinental line on 10 May 1869, Canada and (by dint of their then-governmental ties) Great Britain took this as a challenge for the building of a Canadian transcontinental line. Seen also as a way to unite Canada, the project was undertaken almost immediately.

With such personages as Prime Minister Sir John A MacDonald, millionaire industrialist Cornelius Van Horne and Hudson's Bay Company Commissioner Donald Smith behind the project, it was not lacking in motivation. In fact, the promise of a transcontinental line was the lure with which Prime Minister MacDonald brought British Columbia into the then-new Federation of Canada. The agreement was such that, if the line were completed within 10 years, British Columbia would join the Federation.

The ground-breaking for this line occurred on 1 June 1875, at Fort William, on the Kaministiquia River. By the time that a formal contract for the work was signed on 21 October 1880, 1126 km (700 miles) of line had been built. The Canadian Pacific Railway Company was incorporated on 15 February 1881, and from 2 May 1881 through the end of 1882, four km (2.5 miles) of track were laid per day.

The Prairie Section of the line, as far as Calgary, was completed on 18 August 1883; and the Great Lakes section was completed on 16 May 1885—after much difficulty in laying track over the muskeg bogs and blasting cuts in the solid rock outcroppings north of Lake Superior.

The most difficult section by far was the Mountain Section west from Calgary, through the Rocky and the Selkirk mountain ranges. This line required the construction of towering wooden bridges over mountain gorges—the prime example of which was the 331 meter-long (1086 feet) Mountain

Creek Bridge, in the Selkirks—and the blasting out of many tunnels and cuts in the Rockies and the Selkirks.

The now-famous spiral tunnels at Kicking Horse Pass were necessitated by the steepness of the original line, which was built as an expedient. Where now the line between the tunnels is a diagonal, the original line plunged straight ahead over the Kicking Horse River, descending 1141 feet in seven miles, for a harrowing one-in-32 gradient.

The Selkirks in winter posed an especial hazard, with 321 kph (200 mph) snow avalanches roaring down the slopes, taking men and equipment with them.

Even so, the work was done. Donald Smith drove the last spike at Craigellachie, a camp town in Eagle Pass, British Columbia, on 7 November 1885. In 1889, the luxurious *Imperial Limited* began making regular runs from Montreal to Vancouver, covering the distance in just over four days.

The *Imperial Limited* featured a couple of observation cars with rooftop cupolas for better viewing, and could be said to have pioneered the 'dome car' concept that became so popular in the 1950s. Also, Canadian Pacific used a car with waist-high sidewalls for open-air touring in the Rockies.

In 1919, the luxurious all-sleeper train *Trans Canada Limited* began its service, and the 1920s saw the introduction of such other cross-country services as the *Toronto Express* and the *Mountaineer*. With the 1930s came the *Dominion*, which took over the old *Imperial Limited* service.

A new golden age of Canadian railway travel occurred with the inception of the later, and now justly famous, *Canadian*. With its Scenic Dome cars, a whole realm of sightseeing was opened up. Passengers could view the lush Canadian landscape better than ever before. Lakes, prairies and spectacular mountain vistas now seemed to envelope them, thanks to the Scenic Dome cars.

Near the front of the train was a dome car with first floor service for economy meals at one end, a lounge with bar and kitchen directly beneath the observation dome, and a first-class lounge at the other end. A second dome car was located at the rear of the train, with an observation dome and downstairs lounge, three double bedrooms and a suite of three bedrooms with a private bathroom.

The *Canadian* was of course equipped with a diner and regular sleeper cars. All sleeping compartments aboard the *Canadian* of the 1950s–60s were equipped with three-channel sound. Two of these channels accessed taped music programs, and the third was the public address system.

As with all North American rail passenger lines, both Canadian Pacific and its rival Canadian National were forced to relinquish their badly slumping passenger business to government operation in the 1970s. In 1978, VIA Rail, Canada's answer to the US' Amtrak, merged the passenger service of the two railways.

One of the ramifications of this was that the *Canadian* supplanted all Canadian National offerings as the 'flagship' Canadian trans-continental train. It travelled much of its old route—from Montreal to Vancouver, via Toronto, Sudbury, White River, Winnipeg, Regina, Medicine Hat, Calgary and Revelstoke.

As of 15 January 1990, however, the *Canadian* was consigned to using part of its erstwhile competitor's route. This route had its beginnings as the Grand Trunk Railway, which, at the turn of the century, had a network of rail lines covering Ontario and Quebec. In the interest of competing with the Canadian Pacific, the Canadian government entered into an agreement whereby it would build lines west, connecting with the Grand Trunk's eastern lines. This was to be known as the National Transcontinental Railway, and would stretch between Moncton and Winnipeg.

The Grand Trunk then incorporated a subsidiary, the Grand Trunk Pacific Railway, which built the rest of the line,

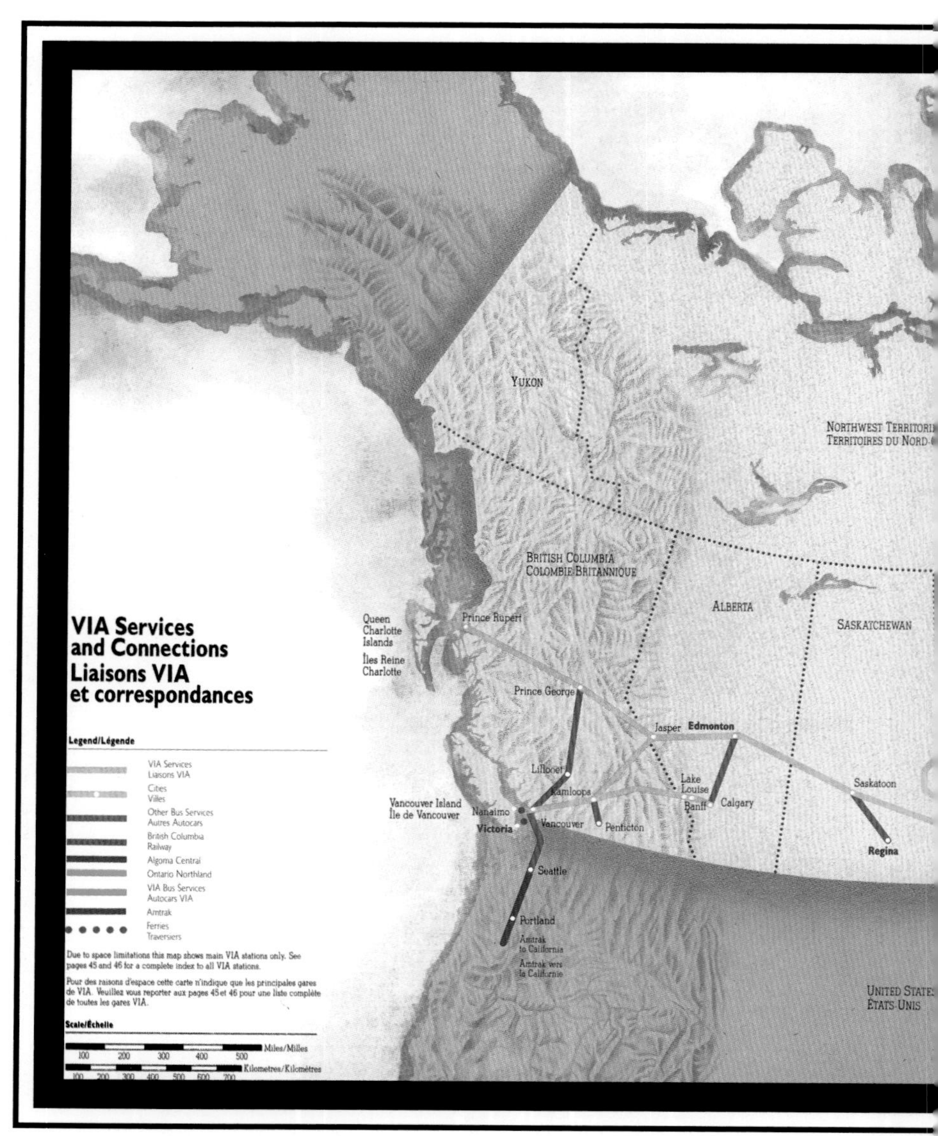

At right: **A vintage open-air tourer, used in the Rockies.** ***Above right:*** **A vintage British Columbia 'local.'** ***Opposite:*** **A poster.**

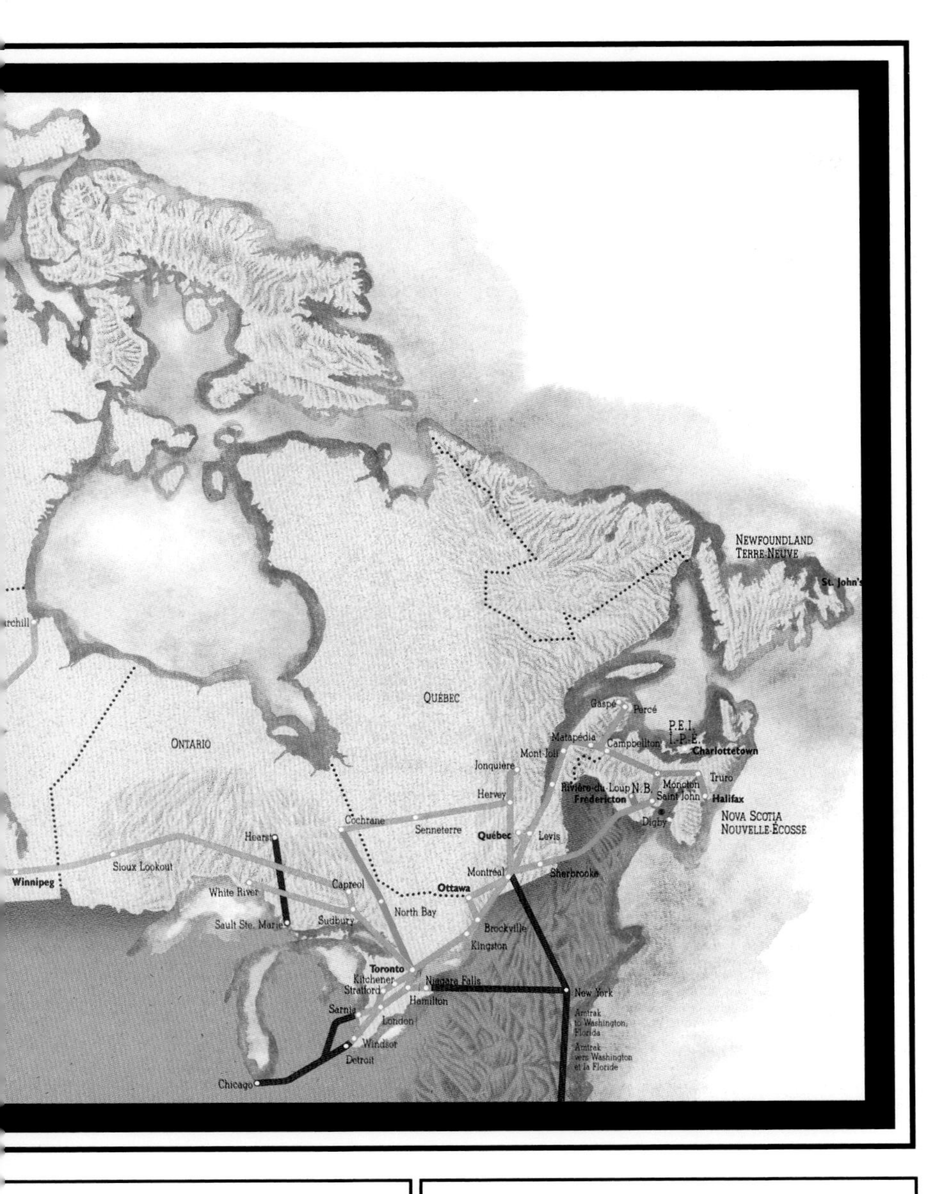

from Winnipeg to Prince Rupert on the Pacific coast. Both projects were begun in 1905. The National Transcontinental was opened in November of 1915, and the Grand Trunk Pacific was completed in September of 1914.

From Winnipeg, this new transcontinental route went by way of Edmonton, and crossed the Rockies at Yellowhead Pass, where it made the lowest crossing of these mountains—5971 km (3711 feet)—and with the easiest grades, of any transcontinental railway. In 1923, Grand Trunk and its subsidiaries were consolidated into the Canadian National Railway, which was destined to be the chief competitor of the Canadian Pacific.

As compared with the pre-1990 routing stated above, the *Canadian* now follows an itinerary that partially follows the old Canadian National route. This begins at Toronto, going on via Capreol, Hornepayne, Winnipeg, Saskatoon, Edmonton, Jasper and Kamloops. Somewhat ironically, this was also partially the route run by the now-discontinued VIA Rail *Super Continental*, itself a half-route (Winnipeg to Vancouver) reprise of the old Canadian National train that had been upstaged by the original *Canadian*.

In 1988, VIA Rail undertook a complete renovation program for all of its passenger stock. In the case of the *Canadian*, this meant a total restoration to 1950s passenger car opulence. The original aura of these cars was lovingly brought into fresh prominence, and even more important, all heating and air conditioning systems were completely replaced with more modern equipment.

The present-day *Canadian* has day coaches in front for short-haul and coach class passengers; 'Daynighter' cars in the midsection, with reclining seats, pull-down trays and overhead lights for economy passengers; and full-scale sleeping cars toward the rear, with private sleeping compartments, section sleeping berths and a drawing room suite.

A coffee shop and cafeteria/lounge car is located near the day coaches, a full dining car is conveniently set in the middle of the train, and a domed observation car with a bar and a lounge is attached to the very rear. This is a train for those making the most of a romantic vacation, and is also a notable favorite with families, though the lone traveler will certainly not lack for conversation or entertainment on the *Canadian*, as the mood on board is generally convivial, and the scenery is spectacular. For that matter, privacy is just a walk to one's large-windowed compartment away.

The single passenger may elect to reserve a single-berth roomette, with a private window seat, a single bed that folds into the wall for day use, and private toilet facilities. The preferred accommodation for couples is the two-person cabin berth, or bedroom, with upper and lower beds, a closet and private toilet facilities.

Another option exists: many families prefer the twin cabin set, with folding doors between the compartments. This allows them to open the doors during the day, creating one large room, and at night, they can close the doors, allowing mother and father and children their respective rooms.

The sleeping compartments are convertible, having an armchair and a comfortable bench seat for day use. When it's time for bed, an upper wall section hinges down to create an upper bunk, and a lower wall section hinges down for a lower bunk, still allowing plenty of access room for a night visit to the lavatory. Beyond the room accommodations, an economy option is provided by the section sleeping berths, with seats facing one another that convert to upper and lower berths, sealed off for sleeping by heavy curtains.

Food is available from a number of sources—snacks and light meals can be obtained from the take-out counter in the observation car or the lounge. More substantial fare is offered to overnight passengers in the diner, where the bill of fare is quite appetizing, and has a straightforward flair that goes hand-in-hand with the pleasurable warmth that this train exudes. A typical breakfast, chosen from the plenitude of offerings on the diner menu, may well include coffee or tea, juice, sausage, eggs, pancakes and potatoes.

Lunch offerings include full meals such as broiled fish with *sauce tartare*, salad and chocolate pudding. The dinner menu allows for such fare as steak, baked potato, apple cobbler and salad, plus drinks. The diner, it should be said, is pleasantly laid out, with clean lines and cheerful coloring, and table settings that make diners feel at home.

The *Canadian* is fully staffed, and the staff members are often quite helpful in unexpected ways. For instance, it is possible to ask a Service Attendant or a Conductor about the operation of the train, and he or she will most likely be able to give a reasonable accounting. Likewise, questions about locations along the route can bring an equally forthcoming response.

With a full-time Service Manager to ensure that all passenger needs are met, the *Canadian* can be said to be one of the most service-conscious rail operations extant today.

The *Canadian*'s route includes historic cities and magnificent scenery. Toronto, the capital of the Province of Ontario, is the starting point for the current itinerary. This city has a large metropolitan area with 2.9 million citizens. Easily discernible above its modern skyline and wide boulevards is the 553-meter-tall (1815.4 feet) Canadian National Tower, which is the world's tallest free-standing structure.

The CN Tower houses a restaurant, a lounge, radio and radar equipment and an observation deck. At its base is CN Hotels' fabulous L'Hotel, a semicircular edifice that contains the utmost in luxury accommodations, and is, with the nationwide string of CN Hotels, included in many of VIA Rail's comprehensive travel packages.

Toronto is situated on the north shore of Lake Ontario, and in its name lies the secret of its wealth: Toronto is the Huron word for 'meeting place.' It was a center of trade long before its incorporation as a city in 1834. Toronto is an extremely clean and cosmopolitan city, and has for years been considered a model urban center.

As passengers while away the day in Toronto, awaiting their late-evening departure time, they might well consider a short trip down the Niagara Peninsula aboard the New

***At right:* A typical western Canadian town by the railway. *Above right:* The *Dominion* at Winnipeg. *Above and below opposite:* Quebec City stations, 1916; Toronto Union Station, 1920s. *Above:* A *Canadian* observation car.**

CANADIAN PACIFIC

CANADI
1416
Canadian Pacific

These pages: **A twin diesel unit of the type used to power the *Canadian* upon its inauguration in 1955. Note the then-current beaver logo and colors. To the left is a *Canadian* dome car.**

SUDBURY JCT
SUDBURY JCT
DOMINION
EXPRESS CO

York City-bound *Maple Leaf*, for a visit to the world-renowned spectacle of Niagara Falls. This LRC train leaves Toronto at 9:35, arriving in Niagara Falls at 11:30. There is plenty of time to visit, as the return *Maple Leaf* swings by Niagara Falls at 18:25, arriving in Toronto at 20:20.

This leaves ample time for dinner and a last-minute check of carry-ons and baggage before departure on the *Canadian*. The *Canadian* runs Tuesdays, Thursdays and Saturdays, leaving from Toronto at 23:30 and arriving four nights and five days later in Vancouver at 8:25. Passengers are allowed to check 45 kg (100 pounds) of baggage for their travel on board, plus carry-ons.

The *Canadian* crosses over its former route at Sudbury Junction, at 7:40 the first morning, continuing north along the old *Super Continental* route to Capreol, a small wilderness hamlet named for a nineteenth-century promoter of railways in the Canadian Great Lakes region. Arrival at Capreol is at 8:15, and passengers have approximately 45 minutes to stretch their legs and explore this town. The next part of the journey takes the *Canadian* through the vast expanse of the Canadian Shield, a region that was thoroughly sculpted by Ice Age glaciers.

Here, sparkling lakes punctuate a beautiful, pristine forest land. Despite its beauty, this area was denounced by early railroad surveyors, as its bedrock is close to the surface, and it is rife with seemingly bottomless pockets of muskeg. This is an area that also has numerous lake resorts and wilderness towns ranging in size from Ycliff, with nine citizens, to Sioux Lookout, with 2495 inhabitants—all of which are served by rail, as highway construction in this area is currently impossible.

The day's journey may be spent sightseeing, reading or playing one of the board games provided by the train's staff. Well over a dozen lakes, nestled amidst the trees, are seen en route to the day's one major stop—a hiatus of 40 minutes that comes at 16:45, when the *Canadian* pulls into Hornepayne, named for EM Hornepayne, one of the builders of the Canadian Northern Railway.

***Above:* The *Canadian* winds through a scenic landscape in 1977.**
***At left:* Sudbury, Ontario, Canadian Pacific station in 1900.**

Hornepayne is a regional center, serving as a hub of sorts for fishing and hunting camps that are filled periodically by those in search of sport in this huge wilderness area. Hornepayne boasts a downtown center that offers schools, shopping, office space and sporting goods—all under one roof.

Departure from Hornepayne is at 17:25. Approximately 100 miles out of Hornepayne, passengers looking west will see Long Lake, one of Canada's largest inland lakes, stretching 45 miles south from the town of Longlac. Near midnight, the train stops at Armstrong, to the south of which lies Lake Nipigon, another major inland lake. Those who enjoy late nights may take this one-half hour opportunity to stretch their legs.

The *Canadian* arrives in Winnipeg at 9:30 the next morning. The stopover lasts until 12:30, allowing ample time to get a sense of this historic city. Located at the junction of the Assiniboine and Red rivers, it is Canada's oldest western city. It was founded in 1812 as Point Douglas by a philanthropic

***Previous pages:* The *Canadian* near Lake Louise. *At left:* Vintage Canadian Pacific mountain service. *Above, all:* VIA Rail crew; passengers; and refurbished regular accommodation.**

Scotsman, Thomas Douglas, Earl of Selkirk, who set it up as a colony in which emigrant Scottish crofters (tenant farmers) could establish their own farms.

With the advent of the railroad in 1885, the bustling settlement became the foundation for the settling of the Canadian west, and was renamed for the Lake Winnipeg, a short distance to the north. Winnipeg is known as 'Canada's answer to Chicago,' and is an active commercial center, with 584,000 citizens. A pleasant city to stroll around, it has wide boulevards, historical buildings and many parks.

From Winnipeg, the *Canadian* follows the second leg of the old *Super Continental* route to Vancouver via Saskatoon, Edmonton and Jasper. The 10 hours' travel between Winnipeg and Saskatoon offers a plethora of Manitoba and Saskatchewan prairie views, including the spectacular panorama that is offered from the tracks riding the north rim of the beautiful Qu'Appelle Valley, with its shining lakes and the Qu'Appelle River meandering lazily across the valley floor.

The *Canadian* pulls into Saskatoon at 22:50 for a layover of 15 minutes, during which passengers making connections to and from Regina may debark or come aboard. After an all-night journey, the *Canadian* arrives at Edmonton at 6:20. This city of 532,246 inhabitants has a plethora of industries, including agriculture, fur, clothing, transportation, natural gas, oil and coal.

Edmonton began as an early fur trading outpost, and has plenty of historical attractions. The interested passenger

***Above:* A *Canadian* travel guide for Japanese tourists. *Opposite:* A station schedule, circa 1986. *Above right, both:* The station at Brantford, Ontario. *At right:* The station at Winnipeg.**

VIA RAIL CANADA
ARRIVALS ARRIVING FROM
ARRIVES ARRIVERA DE
THE ROCKY MOUNTAINEER
AT A
TRAIN NO 101 103 FRI ONLY
JASPER CALGARY BANFF KAMLOOPS
TRACK VOIE 5 OR 6
EXPECTED AT ARRIVERA 1740
DAILY QUOTIDIEN
THE CANADIAN LE CANADIEN
TRAIN NO 1
MONTREAL TORONTO SUDBURY WINNIPEG REGINA CALGARY BANFF LAKE LOUISE KAMLOOPS
TRACK VOIE 6
EXPECTED AT ARRIVERA 1000
TRAIN NO 3
SUPER CONTINENTAL
WINNIPEG SASKATOON EDMONTON JASPER & KAMLOOPS NORTH
TRACK VOIE 6
EXPECTED AT ARRIVERA 1150
WASHINGTON CLOCK WORKS

You'll see more of magnificent Canada from the Scenic Domes of

The Canadian

IN THE DELUXE DINING ROOM CAR you'll enjoy gracious Canadian Pacific service, famous Canadian cuisine. When you're in the mood for a light meal or snack, at popular prices, visit the Skyline Dome Coffee Shop.

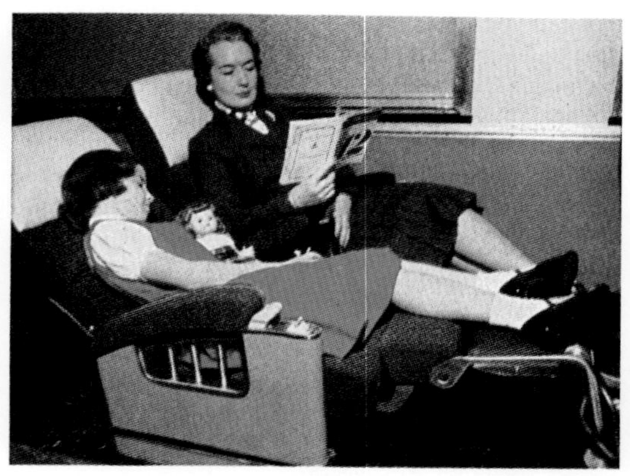

SIT BACK AND RELAX in your reclining coach seat. Adjust full-length leg rests, comfortable foot and head rests to just the positions you want. For your convenience, every seat is reserved in these roomy new-style coaches.

THE MURAL LOUNGE is a perfect spot to enjoy refreshments while you chat with old friends or make new ones. The décor is heightened by a mural specially painted for Canadian Pacific by a distinguished Canadian artist.

THE SPACIOUS MAIN OBSERVATION LOUNGE is a popular spot both day and night. Here you can relax, read, or watch the scenes of majestic beauty flashing by. You'll never forget your Scenic-Dome trip aboard *The Canadian.*

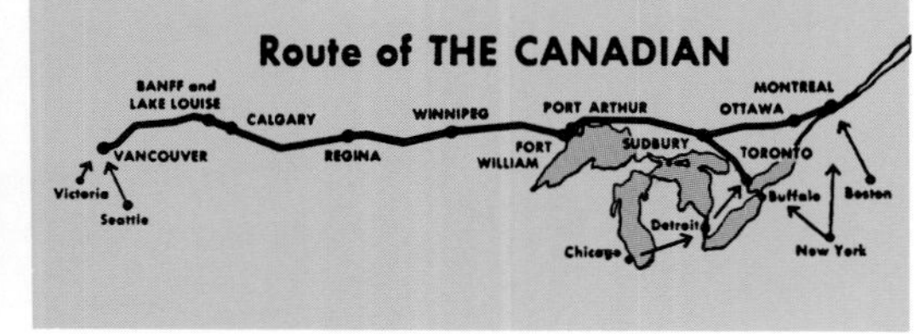

THE CANADIAN OFFERS DAILY SERVICE between Montreal and Vancouver, or Toronto and Vancouver. First class, tourist, or coach, you'll like the spacious accommodations. Ask your travel agent about all-expense tours in the Canadian Rockies or see Canadian Pacific in principal cities in the U.S. and Canada.

Railways · Steamships · Airlines · Hotels · Communications · Express **Canadian Pacific** *World's Greatest Travel System*

may be able to get a sense of this fascinating city before departure on the *Canadian*, at 7:50.

The Rockies are increasingly in evidence as the train nears Jasper—a spectacular mountain resort that was named for a nineteenth century fur trade pioneer, Jasper Hawes. Jasper is surrounded by mountains, and lakes and snowcapped peaks are in abundance. Jasper is also a connection for various bus lines that serve the tourist industry, as well as the VIA Rail *Skeena*, which travels due west to Prince Rupert and Prince George, for an overnight trip of 20 hours and 10 minutes. This one hour and 25-minute stopover is more than enough to make this part of the trip unforgettable. The scenery here is truly breathtaking.

This is the beginning of Yellowhead Pass, the lowest rail crossing of the Rockies in North America. This section of the route has snow-capped peaks on every side for 57 miles, during which the *Canadian* is accompanied on its journey by the Miette River, which flows to the Arctic Ocean, and the Fraser River, which flows to the Pacific Ocean.

Passengers notice these rivers first to the north, and then to the south, of the train. This is an astonishingly beautiful stretch of track, all the way to Kamloops. Between Red Pass and Jackman, Mount Robson—also called 'The Dome'—rises into the clouds, to the north. At 12,972 feet, this is the

***Above:* An advertisement of the 1950s. *Opposite:* Aluminum and ice—the *Canadian* in winter. *At right:* Children aboard a VIA Rail local anxiously await their connection with the *Canadian*.**

VIA

These pages: **The eastbound *Canadian*. Note that the classic *Canadian* unpainted aluminum cars are interspersed with day coaches for local passengers and 'Daynighter' cars for economy fares—both in VIA Rail's standard blue and yellow.**

6531
VIA

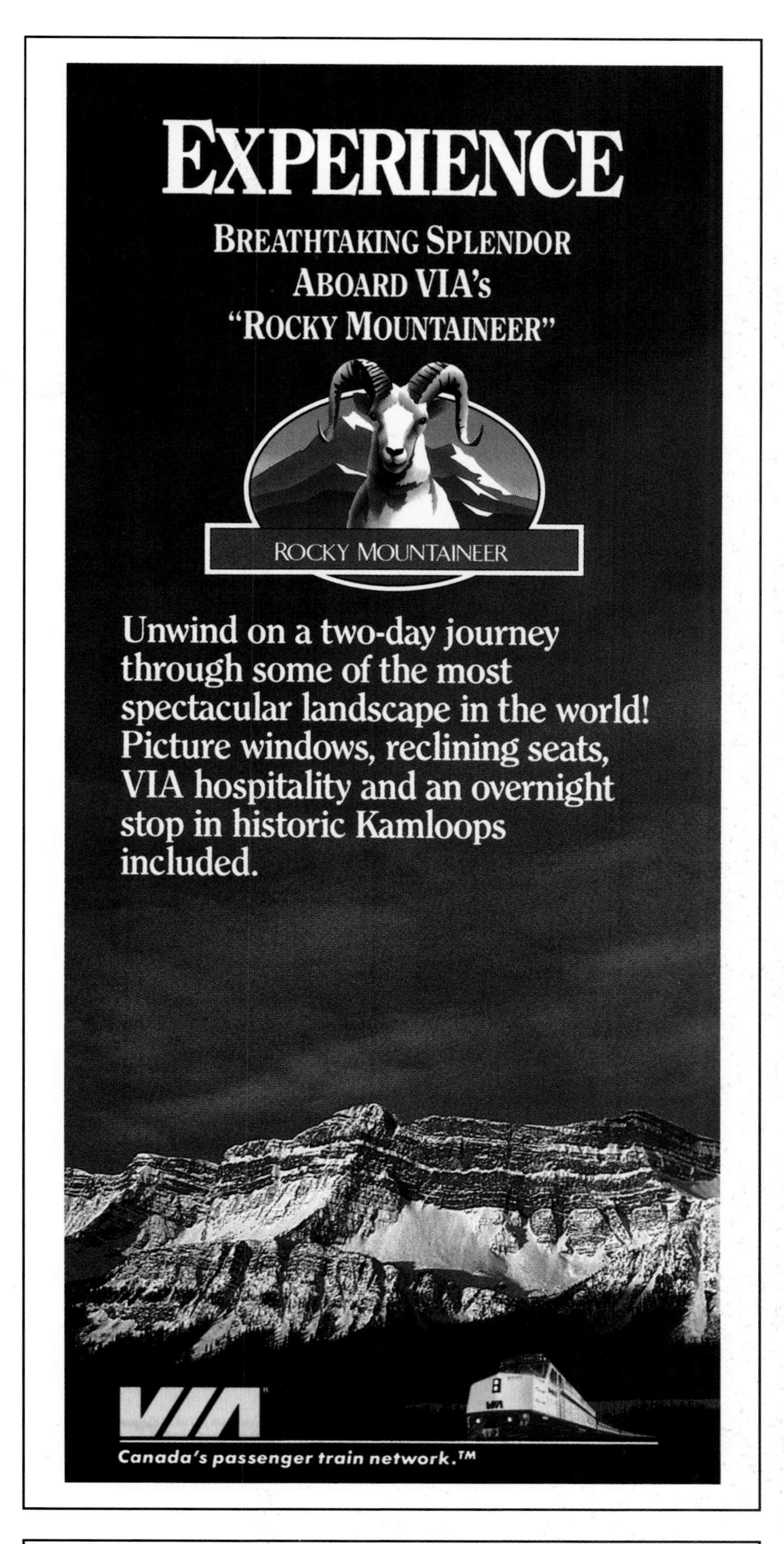

highest peak in the Canadian Rockies. Emerald-green lakes; spectacular waterfalls; spruce, pine and fir forests; and fields of mountain windflowers provide extraordinary vistas for this part of the *Canadian*'s itinerary.

In making this wondrously lovely passage through the mountains, the *Canadian* travels from Alberta to British Columbia, and is hence on the last leg of its journey. The stop in Kamloops takes place at 22:20, and departure is effected 20 minutes later. Kamloops is a Salish Indian word that means 'Meeting of the Waters,' which refers to its location at the fork of the North and South Thompson rivers.

For those fans of moonlit terrain, the next stretch of track, following the Thompson River, passes through rolling, rugged, dusty hills and canyons, accented here and there by a patch of vegetation where irrigation has been successful.

Above: **A brochure.** ***Above left:*** **A** ***Rocky Mountaineer*** **brochure. On the pre-1990** ***Canadian*** **route:** ***At left and opposite:*** **Trainmen at Medicine Hat; and Banff, in the Rockies.**

VIA

These pages: **Medicine Hat, a classic stop on the traditional *Canadian* line. Magnificent Jasper and historic Edmonton are on the current, more northerly, itinerary. Therefore, *Canadian* passengers travel the equally fascinating and spectacular new route with as much excitement as the old.**

The train then follows the powerful Fraser River through its spectacular steep canyon.

As the sun is rising, the *Canadian* traverses a mellow, verdant region of farms and livestock ranches. To the south, it is possible to see the snow-capped cone of Mount Baker—across the border in the state of Washington. Shortly after, the crossing of the Coquitlam River (followed by a sharp turn to the south) is a signal for passengers to say their goodbyes to their new acquaintances and to the fabulous train upon which they have journeyed.

The *Canadian* pulls into Main Street Station, Vancouver, at 8:25 on the fifth day of travel. Vancouver was laid out in 1880, as the western terminus of the Canadian Pacific Railway. Fire destroyed it in 1886, but it was then rebuilt. Spectacularly beautiful, Vancouver is located on a peninsula projecting into the Strait of Georgia, and has 98 miles of water frontage. It is one of North America's premier tourist attractions, with buses, trains and ferries accessing the spectacular forests and mountains of coastal and interior Canada and the US' Pacific Northwest, as well as Vancouver Island.

Even as the westbound *Canadian* is coming into the station, an eastbound train is being prepared for an evening departure for Toronto, scheduled to leave at 21:00 on Thursdays, Saturdays and Mondays—a slight variation from the westbound schedule. As the eastbound passengers mount the steps into the *Canadian's* streamlined aluminum cars, they must know that they are embarking on one of the premier sightseeing tours in all the world, and for the next five days, will be treated with the utmost courtesy aboard a train that has every amenity to make them comfortable.

The *Canadian*. *Above:* Relaxing in the rear observation lounge. *At right, top to bottom:* happy tourists; a Scenic Dome observation deck; awaiting a connection north to the *Canadian*; eager passengers. *Opposite:* The VIA Rail terminal in Vancouver.

NATIONAL
VIA
Budget

VIA

These pages: **Journey's end and journey's beginning: a newly arrived *Canadian* and a soon-to-be eastbound *Canadian* at the VIA Rail/Canadian National Station in Vancouver, BC.**

The USA's Southern Pacific Daylight

*tyle and comfort—in the 1950s there was one US train that was legendary for providing West Coast rail passengers the utmost in modern luxury and refinement: the Southern Pacific **Daylight**. Passengers electing to voyage south from Portland, Oregon—or by connecting service, from Seattle, Washington—could go all the way to Los Angeles, and had a choice of itineraries.*

*The **Daylight** name was actually applied to a number of possible routings availed to the public by the Southern Pacific Railroad. Among these were routes named for their California itinerary. One was an inland route that took its passengers down the San Joaquin Valley, and the other was a coastal route that provided spectacular vistas of the coastal mountains and shoreline. The **Daylights** that took these routes were known respectively as the **Valley Daylight** and the **Coast Daylight**.*

*On the other hand, the **Shasta Daylight** was that which ran from Portland to San Francisco, and was the first Southern Pacific passenger train to be designed especially for diesel power.*

UNION
STATION
X4449
4449
4449

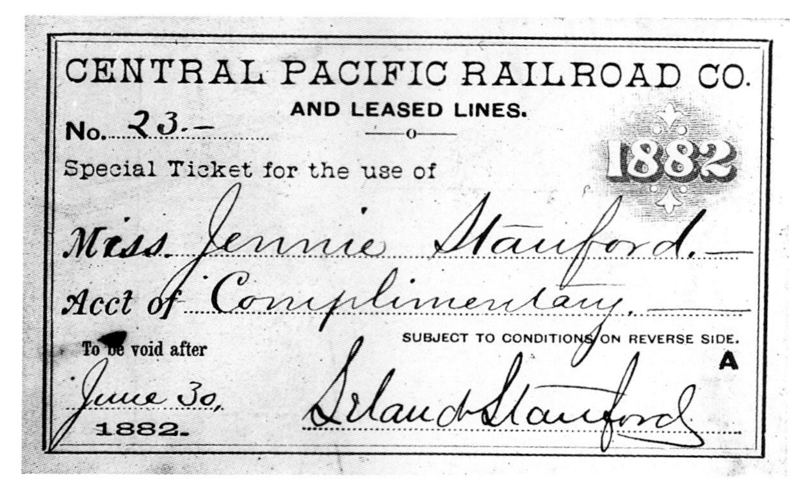

CENTRAL PACIFIC RAILROAD CO.
AND LEASED LINES.
No. 23.-
1882
Special Ticket for the use of
Miss Jennie Stanford
Acct of Complimentary
To be void after
June 30, 1882.
SUBJECT TO CONDITIONS ON REVERSE SIDE.
A
Leland Stanford

The *Daylight* color scheme of red, orange and black lateral stripes was found on all of each train's 12 cars, as well as the sleek 4-8-4 oil burning steam locomotive that headed the *Coast* and *Valley Daylights* in their heyday.

Streaking along one of its several routes, the *Daylight* looked like a landlocked comet with a long, luminous tail of fire; the last thing bystanders saw of the train as it flashed by was the signature red neon 'Daylight' logo on the rounded tail of its observation car.

This magnificent service was not yet dreamed of in 1868, when Southern Pacific Railroad President Timothy Phelps announced his plan to build a railroad from San Francisco to San Diego, and thence eastward to New Orleans. The first step of this bold plan was to buy the San Francisco & San Jose Railroad, an existing line that connected those two cities.

On 25 September 1869, the Central Pacific Railroad, the western segment of the first transcontinental railroad in the US, bought out the Southern Pacific, and the San Francisco-San Diego project continued. The Central Pacific brought its

***Previous page:* A restored *Daylight* 4-8-4 locomotive. *Above:* A yearly pass. *At top:* Building the lines in the Sierra Nevada. *Opposite:* An early Southern Pacific station in Salem, Oregon.**

& DEPOT
STATE HOUSE 3 & DEPOT
SALEM STREET R. W. CO.

transcontinental link to the partnership, as well as the Sacramento Valley Railroad—California's first railroad, which ran from Sacramento to Folsom.

The Central Pacific/Southern Pacific also began construction of rail lines in the San Joaquin Valley, and a rail line north to Redding, which were completed in 1872. By 1874, the line to San Diego had reached Bakersfield, and work commenced on the Tehachapi Loop, which was to create a negotiable gradient over the coastal Tehachapi Mountains, just north of Los Angeles. The line to Los Angeles was completed in 1876, and the first train from San Francisco to Los Angeles was run on September 5 of that year.

In 1884, the complete merger of the Central Pacific and the Southern Pacific Railroads took place, with all operations, including ferry lines, assumed under the name of the Southern Pacific. By this time, passenger trains were running many of the routes. These trains had day cars and section sleepers, with seats that converted into lower berths and upper berths that pulled down from the walls.

A line from Portland, Oregon to Marysville, California had been under construction by the Oregon & California Railroad in 1868. The line crossed the Clackamas River in December of 1869, and was as far south as Eugene by October of 1871. The original management of the Oregon & California went bankrupt in 1872, and the company was taken over by Henry Villard, who succeeded in pushing the line to Ashland, Oregon, near the California border, in 1884. Southern Pacific took over the Oregon & California Railroad when Villard went bankrupt in 1887.

This was called the SP's Siskiyou Line. The Southern Pacific now had rail access from the Pacific Northwest to all more southern points on its many routes, and a traveller could purchase a single ticket and travel from the delta of the Columbia River to the delta of the Mississippi. (The

***Above:* The *Oregon Express* in Sacramento, in 1882. *At right, and above and below opposite:* A poster of the 1950s; *Daylight* route maps. *Extreme opposite:* The rear of a *Daylight* observation car.**

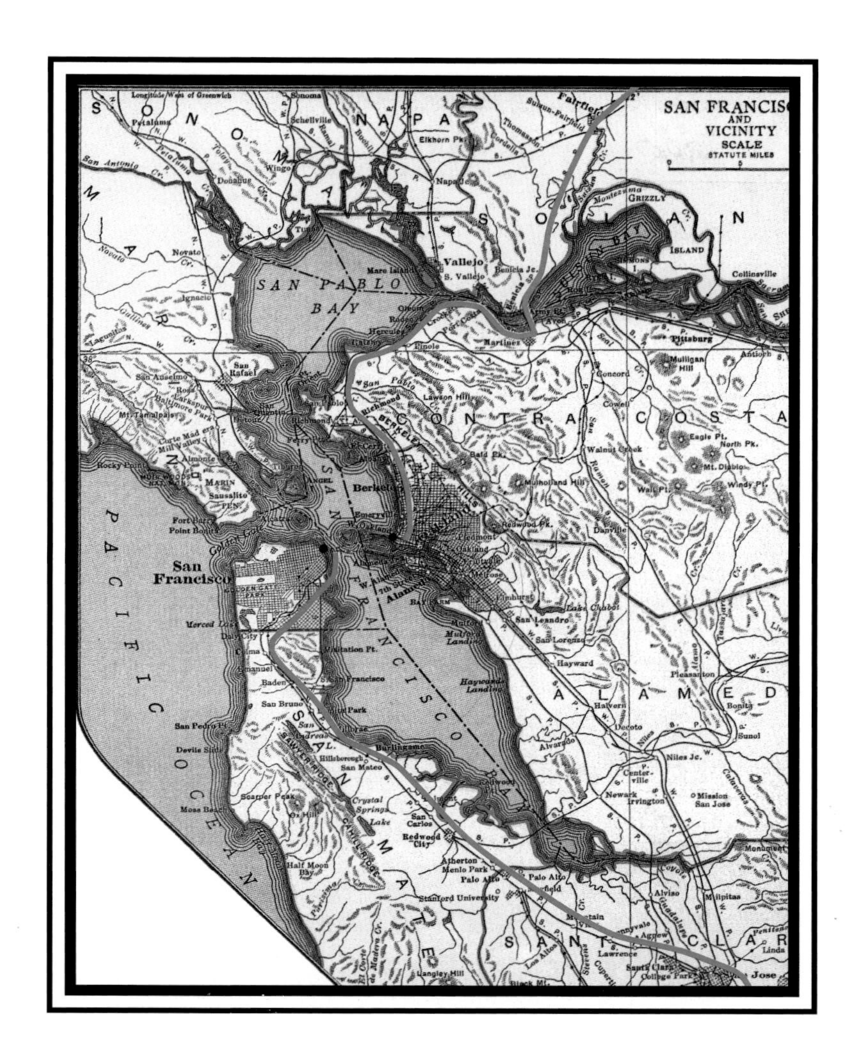
SAN FRANCISCO
AND
VICINITY
SCALE
STATUTE MILES
SONOMA
NAPA
SOLANO
MARIN
SAN PABLO
BAY
CONTRA COSTA
ALAMEDA
SAN FRANCISCO
SAN MATEO
SANTA CLARA
PACIFIC OCEAN
San
Francisco
Berkeley
Vallejo
San Rafael
Sausalito
San Leandro
Hayward
Palo Alto
Stanford University
Redwood City
Half Moon Bay
San Jose

Daylight

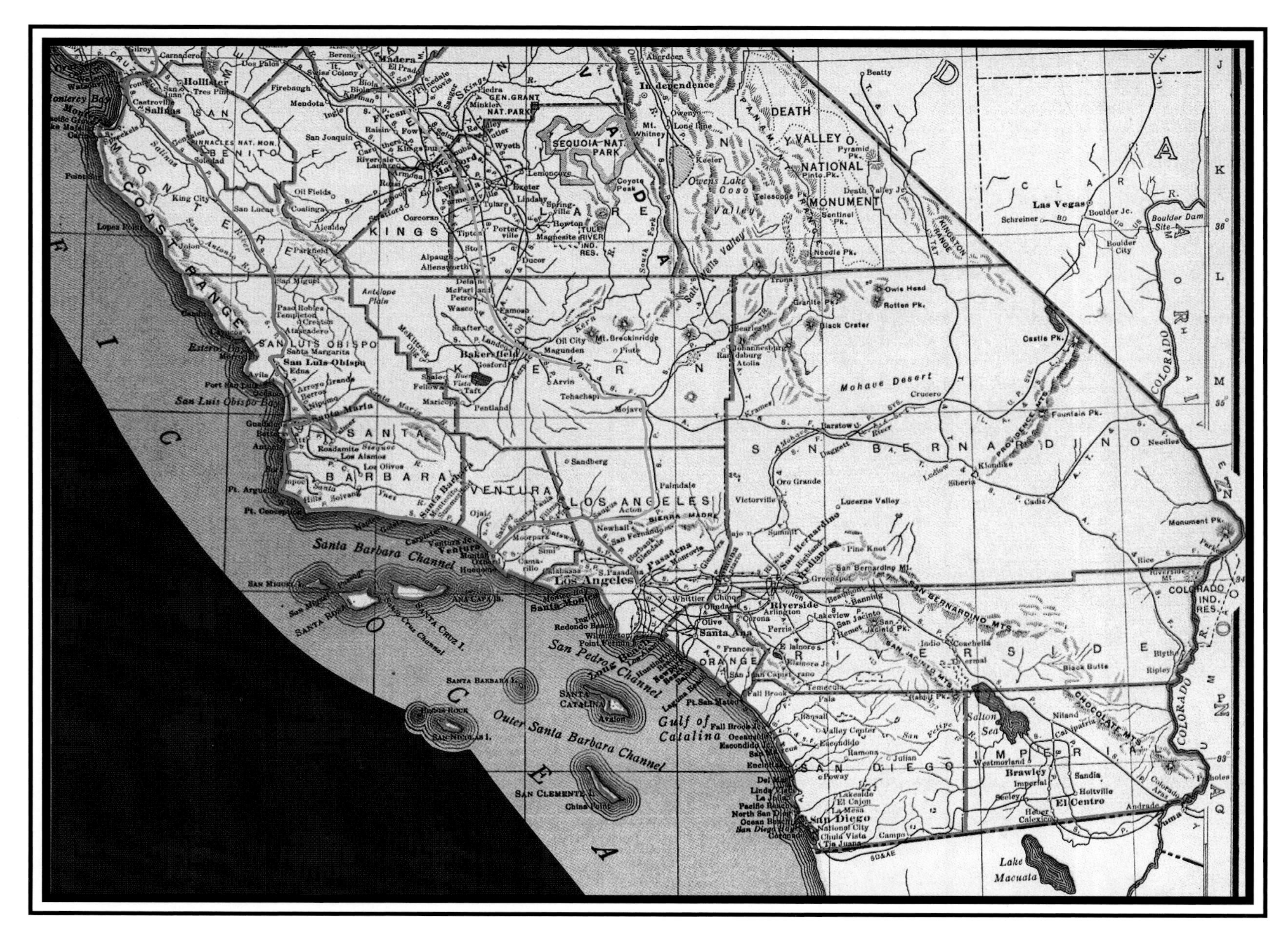
SAN BENITO
MONTEREY
COAST RANGE
KINGS
TULARE
KERN
SAN LUIS OBISPO
SANTA BARBARA
VENTURA
LOS ANGELES
ORANGE
SAN DIEGO
IMPERIAL
RIVERSIDE
SAN BERNARDINO
INYO
DEATH VALLEY NATIONAL MONUMENT
SEQUOIA NAT. PARK
GEN. GRANT NAT. PARK
PINNACLES NAT. MON.
CLARK
NEVADA
ARIZONA
COLORADO R.
Owens Lake
Mohave Desert
Salton Sea
Lake Macuata
PACIFIC OCEAN
Santa Barbara Channel
San Pedro Channel
Gulf of Catalina
Outer Santa Barbara Channel
San Luis Obispo Bay
Hollister
Salinas
Fresno
Bakersfield
Mojave
Barstow
Las Vegas
Independence
Santa Barbara
Ventura
Los Angeles
Pasadena
San Bernardino
Riverside
Santa Ana
San Diego
El Centro
Brawley
Needles
Yuma
Santa Catalina
San Clemente I.
San Nicolas I.

Southern Pacific through route from Los Angeles to New Orleans had been completed on 12 January 1883.)

The first through train from Portland to San Francisco was inaugurated on 17 December 1887. That same year, the Southern Pacific took control of the Southern Pacific Coast Railroad from Felton, in Santa Cruz County, to Oakland. This was extended south from Felton to Los Angeles. The extended route was completed on 31 March 1901, allowing travel from San Francisco to Los Angeles, via San Jose and Santa Barbara, and was known as the Coast Line.

Such fabled passenger express trains as the Southern Pacific's *Overland Limited* and the *Oregon Express* traversed the vast railroad's maze of trackage at the turn of the century. Pulled by 4-4-2 Atlantic-type locomotives, the Southern Pacific deluxe trains of the period typically had Pullman sleepers, convertible for day use; a club car; day cars with carry-on storage above the seats; a diner; and a mail-baggage car.

The Southern Pacific continued to develop and expand its lines, double-tracking and improving wherever it could. In 1922, the immediate predecessors of the *Daylights* began making their runs from San Francisco to Los Angeles and points beyond. These were the *Owl*, via Bakersfield and Fresno; the *Tehachapi*, via Visalia, Los Banos and Tracy; and the *Valley Flyer*, via Bakersfield, Modesto and Los Banos.

The *Shasta*, via Seattle, Tacoma and Portland; the *Oregonian*, via Seattle, Tacoma and Portland; the *California Express*, which ran much the same route; and the *San Francisco Express*, via Seattle, Portland and Klamath Falls, were the precursors of the *Daylights* that ran to the Northwest. The 270-mile Cascade Line paralleling the Siskiyou Line

***Above and at right:* The Southern Pacific's *Overland Limited* crosses Utah's Great Salt Lake on the Lucin Cutoff viaduct. Such great early trains were the precursors of the *Daylights*.**

through the Oregon Cascade Range was opened for passenger traffic in 1927.

Such developments opened the way for the Golden Era of Southern Pacific train travel. In 1936, Southern Pacific entered into a cooperative agreement with the Union Pacific and the Chicago Northwestern Railroad to jointly operate the *City of San Francisco*, between Chicago and San Francisco. This was the first streamlined all-diesel passenger express in the western US, and was billed as the longest, most luxurious and fastest of them all, attaining 176 kph (110 mph) at points on its itinerary.

The *City of San Francisco* set a tone that was to influence all Southern Pacific passenger trains to follow. The all-steel cars were named for places in San Francisco—*Market Street*, *Seal Rock*, *Chinatown*, *Telegraph Hill*, *Union Square*, and so on. With lounge car, observation car, an immaculate diner, a tavern car and a variety of first-class sleeping accommodations as well as a sophisticated communications system, this was a pace-setting train, to be sure.

The cars were pure Art Deco, with French green, Nantes blue, apricot, jonquil, smoke gray and beige interiors. Chrome-trimmed tables and crescent leather booths highlighted the lounge car; the tavern car had mirror tables and soft lighting. All was air conditioned. The premier accommodation was a private suite that slept four and had its own lounge and bathroom.

In 1937, the Southern Pacific introduced its own streamliners, which included the *Sunbeam*, with service to Dallas and Houston, and the fabulous *Daylight*, from San Francisco to Los Angeles. Accommodations were of the utmost refine-

Southern Pacific stock, 1870–1900. *Opposite:* A lounge. *Above and at right:* Pullman sleepers. *Above opposite:* Second class.

6051
X6051
RADIO EQUIPPED
SOUTHERN
LINES
PACIFIC
F

These pages: **Diesels representing three prestigious railroads of the American West in the 1950s—the Southern Pacific, the Union Pacific and the Santa Fe. In 1936, the Southern Pacific began the joint running of the diesel-only *City of San Francisco* with the Union Pacific and the Chicago Northwestern.**

ment, from the painted trim of slender leaf-and-stalk borders with tiny quatrefoil motifs, to the soft velour upholstery and the clean, Bauhaus-inspired lines of the cars.

On the *Daylight*, in addition to a cabin sleeper car, there was a diner; a lounge/observation car with large windows and rotating, tiltable seats; and section sleeper cars with amazingly luxurious convertible upper and lower berths, shielded for privacy by satiny curtains. There were also day cars with large windows and recliner seats; and a postal car.

The observation/lounge car rode at the end of the train, and featured the large windows and a panoramic field of vision out the rounded rear windows at the end of the car. One could take a shower on board if one wanted to, and there was every kind of amenity for carrying out leisure activities or company business.

Bauhaus indeed, with a touch of Art Deco, the decor was what one would expect in a modern luxury hotel, and meals could be taken either in the passenger cars or in the diner, which featured shining white linens and silver tableware buffed to a soft, lustrous tone. This was complete with a full complement of gastronomic delights that were represented in smaller portions on the children's menu. The *chef de train* had a fully-equipped kitchen with which to please the passengers' palates.

***Above:* A 1930s station schedule. *At right:* A barbershop on the Pullman car *Olympian*. *Opposite:* A *Daylight* section berth.**

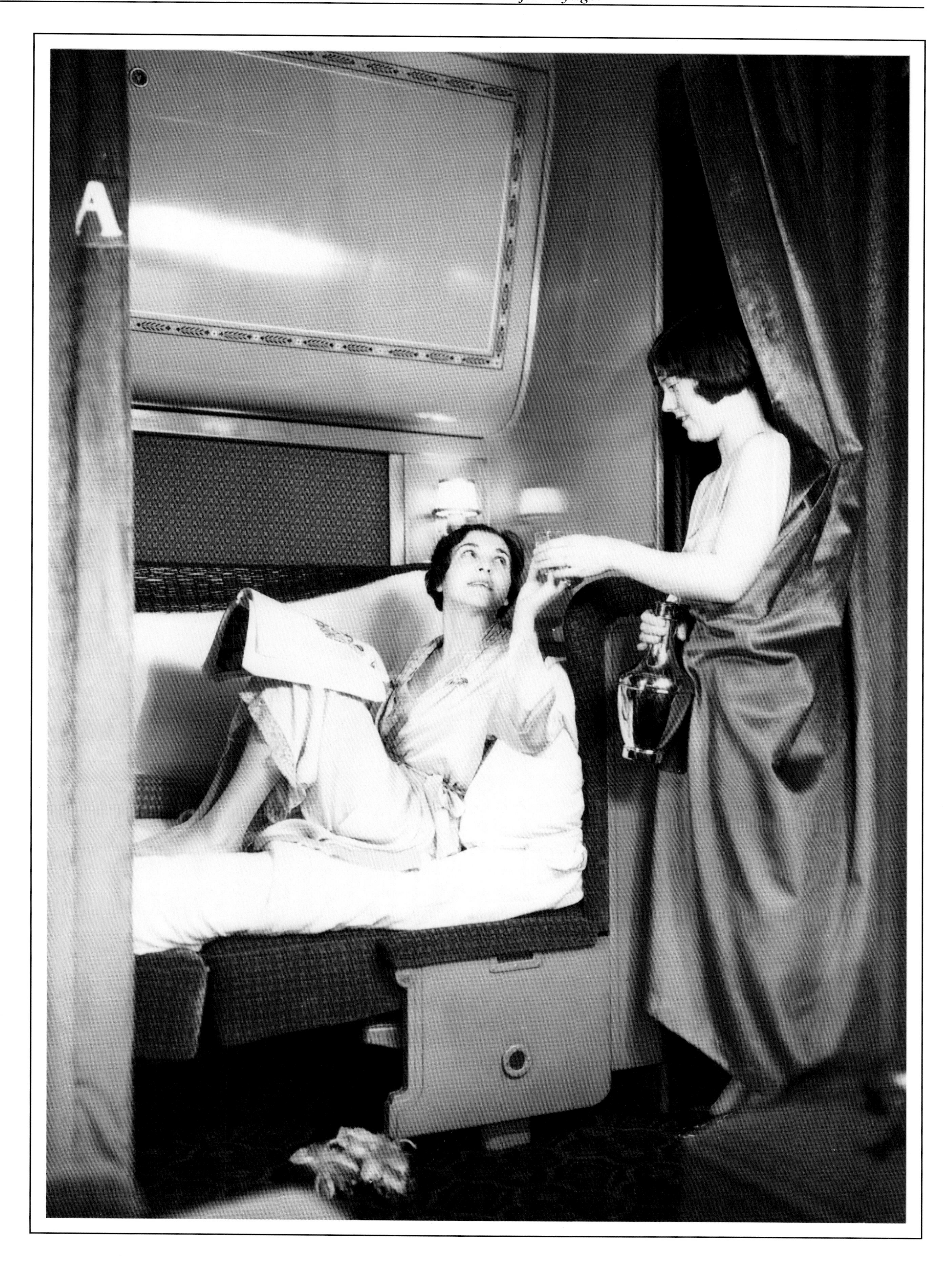
A

Breakfast was likely to be any of a variety of sausage, bacon, eggs any style, fried potatoes, French toast, pancakes, juice, coffee or tea. The lunch menu would present such entrées as a tasty clam chowder, a variety of sandwiches, including the 1950s-favorite club sandwich, soup and a number of desserts and beverages. Dinner would give the passenger a choice of steak, braised sirloin tips, chicken or seafood; with vegetables (asparagus or peas on the side in a savory cream sauce); a choice of baked or mashed potatoes; and a gelatin fruit dessert, ice cream or cobbler after that.

The staff was smiling and friendly, and provided a wide range of services. For instance, if you were a new parent, a steward would fill and warm baby's bottle for you.

***At right:* A *Daylight* observation car. This is part of an entire *Daylight* train that has been restored for exhibitions. *Above:* A promotional brochure for *Daylight* service of the 1940s.**

Daylight
GS 1290

LOCAL

THROUGH

In 1945, Southern Pacific introduced a swarm of new passenger services to accomodate what was anticipated as a surge in postwar business. This business was a terrible disappointment, thanks to competition from the airplane and the automobile. However, 1948 saw the introduction of the *Golden State*, from Tucson to Chicago; 1950 brought the *Sunset Limited*, which ran from New Orleans to Los Angeles in 42 hours. The all-streamlined *Cascade*, following the Cascade Line, was introduced that same year.

Among these enhancements were expansions of the *Daylight* schedules. In 1949, the *Shasta Daylight* and its predominantly night-running twin, the *Shasta Starlight*, were introduced on the line from Portland to San Francisco. These trains made the run south in 16 and one-half hours.

Previous pages: **The SP ticket counter at the Palace Hotel, San Francisco, circa 1920. *Daylight* restored: a cook *(above)*, and dinner service *(opposite)*. *At right:* The *Shasta Daylight*, 1951.**

Also, passengers had a choice of taking the *San Joaquin Daylight* inland through the agriculturally picturesque San Joaquin Valley, or the spectacular *Coast Daylight* from San Francisco to Los Angeles.

Passengers boarded the *Shasta Daylight* in the morning at Portland, at 7:45. In the early 1950s, Portland was in the full bloom of its renown as 'The City of Roses.' Nearly every home in the city grew roses—and Peninsula Park, with its more than 1000 varieties of roses, was a revelation.

In the morning light, the *Shasta Daylight* headed out of Portland, moving out through the Coast Range foothills. Soon the windows of the swivel-seat-equipped observation coaches were full of Pacific Northwest verdure. Hillsides and evergreens, and the occasional glimpse of the meandering Willamette, formed a pleasant background for passengers' reflections as the train eased itself into the first leg of its journey.

Just before 9:00 the train pulled into Salem, Oregon, the state capital, a small city of perhaps 89,000 that is, like Portland, located on the Willamette River. Interesting stops like this helped to add additional variety to the journey to San Francisco. The stops along the line to the California border included Albany, Eugene and Klamath Falls.

Soon enough, the observant traveller would discern that the *Shasta Daylight* followed the Willamette River practically all the way to Crescent Lake, and might have wished to view that leg of the trip from the observation car.

***Above:* Southern Pacific express service in 1936. *At right:* A railway post office car of the *Shasta Daylight*, in 1950.**

SOUTHERN PACIFIC
SP 6600
42

4449
4449

These pages: **A closeup of a classic, Southern Pacific 4-8-4 steam locomotive in *Daylight* coloration, with a whole string of *Daylight* cars behind it.**

The train would be full of businessmen, and just the sort of optimistic young couples advertisers had done everything to persuade of their services, as well as older families out for a lark. It was probable that not a few of the passengers were headed for Southern California in hopes of taking advantage of the cheap land and abundant opportunities that that area then offered.

Therefore, the mood on board the *Daylight* of the early 1950s was great optimism. Adding to this were the solicitous stewards and stewardesses, who were ever-attentive to passenger needs.

The mountainous forestland, the Klamath Lake panorama and Klamath Falls would offer scenes of great natural beauty, as would the awesome spectacle of Mount Shasta rising out of the foothills to the right of the train, dwarfing primordial evergreen forests. Not long afterward, the train headed into Dunsmuir, California, at 17:00 that afternoon.

Evergreen forests and mountain terrain still filled the windows, and on toward Redding, the rugged countryside took on a pristine beauty, with oak forests and achingly pure

Opposite: **A *Daylight* maintenance crew of 1943. The *Daylights* were symbolic of ambitious operations: witness the SP Houston station *(above)* in the 1930s. *At right:* Baggage handling.**

4365
MEN
AT
WORK

coloration—the sort of landscape that has been so often called 'God's Country.'

Then the *Daylight* flew on through the fertile expanses of the Sacramento Valley, running fast and true for the Bay Area and San Francisco. Night began to fall, and the miles ticked by with the steady rythms of wheels on track, right on into Oakland. Passengers going farther south caught the ferry in the morning, and boarded the *Coast Daylight* at San Francisco Station. San Francisco in 1950 was a great port city—unlike the present day, in which port activity has all but vanished, and the looming shapes of highrises pronounce its new life as a banking and financial center.

Coming across the Bay by ferry in 1950, one would have been confronted by a city that seemed entirely painted

***Above, both:* Brochures. *At right:* Artwork of a northbound *Coast Daylight*. *Opposite:* A restored *Coast Daylight* exhibition train.**

JOIN US IN THE DINING CAR

Beverages

FROM THE BAR

Wine (A Split Bottle) 2.25
■ Chardonnay (A Dry White)
■ Cabernet Sauvignon (A Classic Red)
■ White Zinfandel (A Delicate Blush)
Cold Beer 2.00
Soda ■ Diet Soda .... .75

Major credit cards are accepted in the diner. Prices include all state and local taxes.

For lighter fare, plan to visit our snack car. The snack car features snacks, sweets and your favorite beverages. We also sell postcards, playing cards, lapel pins* and blankets.

*On selected trains.

Amtrak®

WELCOME ABOARD

SOUV S-89

JOIN US IN THE DINING CAR

Breakfast

GOOD MORNING!

We invite you to start the day with a hearty breakfast from the menu below. Please check your choices.

All breakfast selections are served with a choice of chilled orange, apple, tomato juice or a cup of fresh fruit and coffee, tea, milk or decaffeinated coffee.

BREAKFAST SELECTIONS

Two Eggs 3.50
Served with potatoes.
■ Up ■ Over ■ Scrambled
Three Buttermilk Pancakes 3.50
■ Plain or ■ with Fruit Topping
Old-Fashioned Railroad French Toast 3.50
■ Plain or ■ with Fruit Topping
The above selections served with breakfast meats ... 4.75
■ Four Strips of Crisp Bacon
■ Three Grilled Sausage Links
■ Grilled Ham Slice

LIGHTER FARE

Hot or ■ Dry Cereal with milk and breakfast breads ... 2.75
With breakfast meats 4.00
■ Bacon Strips ■ Sausage Links ■ Ham Slice

Amtrak®

WELCOME ABOARD

white, and elevated and declined gracefully on the slopes of its hills. The structures were generally low, not more than a few stories, like a close-fitting blanket on the landscape. San Francisco then seemed a magnification of those pristine, whitewashed fishing villages that are found everywhere around the Mediterranean.

The *Coast Daylight* departed San Francisco in the morning, at approximately 8:00, on the second leg of this trip to Los Angeles. It would take a good bit of the day. From San Francisco, the *Coast Daylight* passed through the sunny, fertile reaches of the Salinas Valley.

Then the train went upgrade into the rugged Santa Lucia Mountains, breached the Cuesta Pass, and coming downgrade, rounded a horseshoe curve into San Luis Obispo.

From San Luis Obispo to Santa Barbara, the *Coast Daylight* ran along California's magnificent coastline, where the

The Amtrak version: Superliner *Coast Starlight*'s two-story diner, *right*, contrasts with Amtrak Metroliner stock, *opposite*.

JOIN US IN THE DINING CAR

Lunch

GOOD AFTERNOON!

We are happy to serve you today. A full morning of scenic viewing is sure to have given you an appetite for lunch. Please check your choices.

All luncheon selections are served with a chocolate brownie or cup of fresh fruit and your choice of coffee, tea, milk or decaffeinated coffee.

LUNCHEON SELECTIONS

The Late Riser 3.50
An omelet prepared in the Chef's own style garnished with crisp lettuce and tomato slices and steak fried potatoes.

The Beefburger 4.75
■ Plain or ■ with Cheddar Cheese
Served with cole slaw, kosher pickle spear and steak fried potatoes.

Grilled American Cheese 3.50
Your choice of ■ White or ■ Wheat
With ■ Bacon Strips or ■ Sliced Ham 4.75

The Chef's Sandwich 5.00
Your Attendant will describe today's selection.

OTHER FARE

The Crock Pot Selection 5.00
Each trip we feature a unique pasta combination. Your Attendant will describe this to you.

Amtrak's Salad Platter 5.00
Prepared and garnished in our own style. Your Attendant will describe this to you.

CHILDREN'S MENU

The Sloppy Joe Sandwich 3.50
Prepared on a bun and served with steak fried potatoes, ■ Milk or ■ Juice and choice of ■ Chocolate Brownie or ■ Fruit Cup

Amtrak

WELCOME ABOARD

JOIN US IN THE DINING CAR

Dinner

GOOD EVENING!

What better way to end a day of relaxing amid America's rolling panorama than with an evening meal from our menu of entrees to please the traveler's appetite. Please check your choices.

All dinners include our house salad with choice of dressing Ranch, Caesar, French, dinner breads with butter, dessert and choice of coffee, tea, milk or decaffeinated coffee.

DINNER SELECTIONS

The Day's Chicken Selection 9.50
The Seafood Catch 10.00
Our Chef's Special 11.00
These are prepared by our Chefs onboard and served with potatoes du jour and garden vegetables.
■ Rice is offered in place of potatoes with some selections. Your Dining Car Attendant will describe the dinner selections.

OTHER FARE

The Vegetarian 8.00
Each trip we feature a meatless entree. Your Attendant will describe this to you.

Grilled New York Strip Steak 12.50
10 oz. boneless center cut prepared as you like it.
■ Rare ■ Medium ■ Well Done
Served with mushroom caps and baked potato.

Boneless Prime Rib of Beef, Au Jus 12.50
Served with baked potato and garden vegetables.

CHILDREN'S MENU

Grilled Chicken Cutlet 4.25
Lightly breaded and served with the day's potato, vegetable and milk or chilled juice.

DESSERTS

■Apple Pie ■Apple Pie with Cheddar Cheese
■Specialty Cake or Pastry ■Fruit Pie
■Cheesecake ■Plain or ■Topped with Fruit Sauce

WELCOME ABOARD

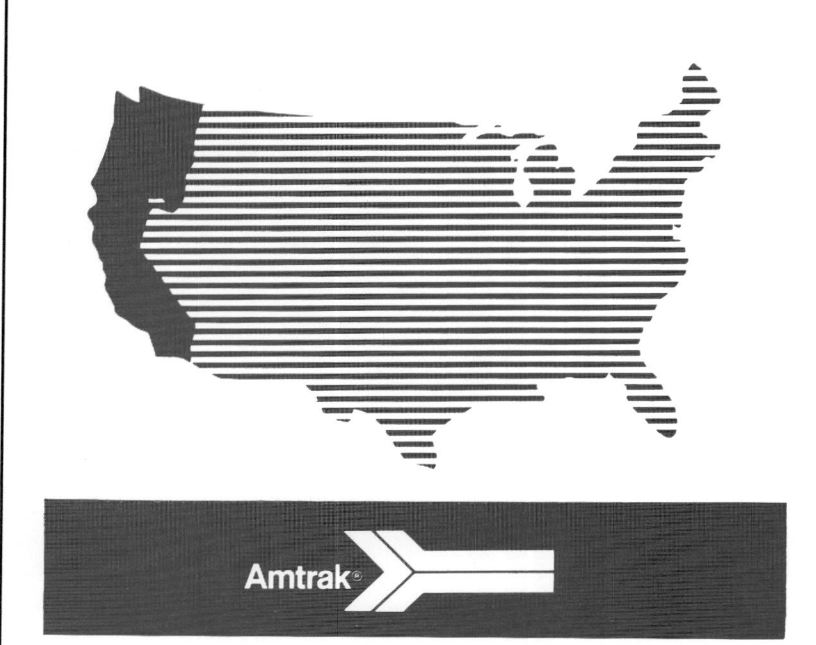

Pacific Ocean sculpts the western edge of the North American continent. Rugged coastal hills; magnificent rock cliffs and sandy beaches; and Southern California flora combined with the awesome grandeur of the Pacfic Ocean to make this part of the *Coast Daylight* route one of the most spectacular in the world.

From Santa Barbara, the train bore inland once more, rising up the western flanks of the Tehachapi Mountains to Santa Susana Pass, and coming down into the San Fernando Valley, pulling into that mecca of movie-making, Los Angeles, that evening.

Unfortunately, rail travel in the US suffered tremendously from the mid-1950s through the 1960s, by dint of competition from the autombile and the airplane. The service on the

At right:* An Amtrak Superliner, with its high-level cars, rounds a scenic bend. *Opposite:* Boarding the *Coast Starlight.

trains became ever more spartan and rundown, due to massive operating deficits. On 1 May 1971, Amtrak, the US federal government's passenger rail service assumed control of the Southern Pacific's passenger lines, trimming them down severely.

The once-proud *Daylights* were consolidated into a single service, which is named the *Coast Starlight*. This train offers both cabin and coach accommodation. Amtrak cabins are of four types—the premier setup being a two-berth unit, convertible for day use, with its own bathroom and shower. The least cabin accommodation is a convertible day/night room, with toilet and washroom facilities at the end of the car.

The *Coast Starlight* also offers a high-level diner, and a high-level observation car with a first-floor bar and entertainment such as recorded music and motion pictures. This train runs a daily schedule of 32 hours and 50 minutes from Seattle to Los Angeles, and takes five minutes more to run the return trip. The itinerary is as follows. From Seattle, the *Coast Starlight* departs at 10:40, and runs via Portland, Sacramento, Oakland, San Jose and Santa Barbara, arriving in Los Angeles at 19:30 on the second day.

There are only two stops en route—at Portland and Oakland, for 15 and 20 minutes, respectively. Accommodation on the *Coast Starlight* should be reserved.

***Above opposite:* San Luis Obispo. *At right and above:* Aboard the *Coast Starlight*. *Opposite:* A re-enactment of a *Daylight* run.**

SAN LUIS OBISPO

DANGER
220
VOLTS

These pages: **The highly adequate Amtrak Superliner *Coast Starlight* stops at San Luis Obispo, just as did its glorious Southern Pacific predecessor. In contrast to this train's high-level cars, there is (as we have previously intimated), a completely refurbished, classic *Daylight* train that is maintained in Portland, Oregon, for exhibition purposes only.**

Amtrak
39958 Coach
Coach 34045

A Tour of the USA on Great American Trains of the 1950s

*ppropriately, the 1950s is regarded as the last decade of the Golden Age of rail passenger travel in the United States. It was possible to cross the United States by a number of different and exciting passenger routes, both north to south and east to west. There were 650 'name' trains, run by independent but interconnected American railroads in the mid-1950s. These trains had such appellations as the **Olympian Hiawatha**, the **North Coast Limited**, the **Twentieth Century Limited**, the **Coast Daylight**, the **Shawnee**, the **Wolverine**, the **Panama Limited** and the **California Zephyr**.*

On a journey from California to New York and back, a passenger could ride as few as two, or as many as nine or more premier trains across 22 states, visiting 10 state capitals (and Washington, DC), top the Continental Divide on a summit 3115 meters (10,221 feet) high, ride a glass bubble 'Vista-Dome' through a precipitous chasm 610 meters (2000 feet) deep and dine regally on fresh Rocky Mountain trout, Kansas City beef, Maine lobsters and Oregon salmon.

The trains themselves were spectacular, powered by streamlined Alco or Baldwin or EMD diesels, pulling with seeming effortlessness a string of streamlined cars: the diner, glittering with silverware glimpsed through the spotless windows; the observation cars, with soft lights on muraled walls; and the Pullmans with porters shaking out snowy linen—not to mention the glass-topped dome cars. These were variously called Vista-, Strata- or Astra-Domes, and glowed softly above the roofs of coaches and lounge cars, as they swept past.

There were literally tens of thousands of possible combinations of routes, perhaps as many as 100,000, the vast majority at no extra fare. This didn't include innumerable scenic side trips, most of which were then possible at little or no additional cost.

In the 1950s, it cost less than US $145 to make a round trip by coach between New York City and any Pacific Coast terminal (Seattle, Portland, San Francisco, Los Angeles, San Diego), or about US $60 additional for first class (sleepers or parlor cars) plus Pullman charges and tax, and it cost no more to expand the round trip into any of thousands of big circles.

Suppose, for example, a traveller started from New York City. One might go west via the Great Lakes, Chicago, Minneapolis-St Paul, the Dakotas, Montana, and Idaho to Seattle; skirt the Pacific Ocean southward to San Diego; return east along the Mexican border through the Southwest and along the Gulf Coast to New Orleans and Mobile; and angle up to

Previous page: **One of the greatest, the *City of San Francisco.* *Above:* Sightseeing in a dome car amidst the Rockies. *At right and opposite:* Advertisement and artwork for dome car travel.**

many travelers prefer to take the train
between the West Coast and Chicago or St. Louis
in this age of space travel

Because just riding Union Pacific's Domeliners to and from Chicago, Kansas City or St. Louis is an extra two day vacation—restful and thoroughly enjoyable.

Next trip, try it yourself. Take the time to relax and unwind. For business or vacation travelers arriving refreshed, ready for work or play, is a good investment.

Spacious Pullman rooms provide complete privacy when you want it or you may join congenial groups in the Lounge or Dome cars. Mealtimes are happy events in both the Diner or the exclusive Dome Dining Car.

Family Fares apply to husband and wife traveling together or when one or both parents accompany the children.

Low Coach Fares provide savings, your own reserved seat, access to the Dome Coach, Lounge and Dining Cars. Generous baggage allowance on all tickets.

OMAHA 2, NEBRASKA

UNION PACIFIC RAILROAD

Early Reservations are advisable. Call any Union Pacific office.

New York via Atlanta, Washington, Baltimore and Philadelphia. Furthermore, it might take six months to make such a journey if the traveller stopped off whenever and wherever he felt like it.

A less comprehensive, yet still fulfilling, round trip, starting and finishing in San Francisco, would take just two weeks in travelling time, including sightseeing stopovers. During this time the traveller would meet a wide variety of friendly co-travellers, would eat like royalty in numerous excellent on-board diners, and would telephone whomever he pleased from a train.

It was even possible to sit in a barber chair, getting a haircut on a train going 127 kph (79 mph), and several trains had an on-board public secretary, to which passengers could dictate letters and business correspondence for free. Most trains had in-cabin music programs and radio access that could be switched on and off at will by passengers.

The first train on our smaller proposed itinerary would be

***At right and opposite:* Passengers at old Third Street Station, San Francisco. *Above:* The B&O station at Harper's Ferry.**

SHASTA ROUTE
PORTLAND · SAN FRANCISCO
Southern Pacific
THE NEW STREAMLINER
CITY OF SAN FRANCISCO
SOUTHERN ARIZONA
DUDE RANCHES & RESORTS
Southern Pacific
Southern Pacific

These pages: **Indicative of the decline of rail travel is this once proud diner car that has been converted into a diner of another kind. This situation is a wry echoing of the excellent cuisine offered by the great American trains of the 1950s.**

F E
OPEN
531
CLOSED
WEDNESDAYS

UNION PACIFIC
NORTH WESTERN
102
SF-1

the *California Zephyr*, which was spectacularly streamlined, with five Vista-Domes. Jointly owned and operated by the Burlington, Rio Grande and Western Pacific railroads, the *California Zephyr* plied the rails between Chicago and Oakland, with a through sleeper to New York, in the early 1950s.

Seated in this train's sunny Vista-Dome, passengers had a commanding view of the morning countryside as it rolled past. In the early afternoon, the *California Zephyr* bored into one of the far West's wonderlands, the Feather River Canyon, for the long ascent of the Sierra Nevada. Wholly unlike travel in a regular car, the Vista-Dome accessed scenery not only to the sides and the front and rear, but also allowed viewing upward, and gave passengers a panorama that made them feel that they were truly amidst the wonders that they viewed.

***At left:* Diesels for the *City of San Francisco* (left) and the *City of Denver*. *Above:* In a dome car. *At top:* An advertisement.**

The *California Zephyr*'s Vista-Dome revealed the famous canyon in all its majesty—the frothing river beside the tracks, the lofty evergreen slopes and craggy ramparts soaring to the blue wedge of sky far above. Passengers might also have noticed a peculiar, fence-like string of wires beside the tracks and asked what it was. A helpful steward would be glad to answer that this was a landslide detector. Any falling rocks would break one of the detector's wires before reaching the rails and every train would stop automatically until the line was inspected and cleared.

A myriad of such safety devices helped to account for the railroads' remarkable safety record of fewer than one fatality in the equivalent of 100,000 round trips coast to coast. It was a record that is matched tenfold by the airlines today, but not by the airlines in the early 1950s and before.

The recorded musical programs over the public address system during the day had been interrupted occasionally by a lilting feminine voice announcing sights of interest. A traveller might chance to meet the source of that voice, a real, live 'Zephyrette,' who, like today's airline stewardesses, was 'getting paid to see the world.'

If a *California Zephyr* passenger decided to stop over in Salt Lake City, only a minute was required for the conductor to rearrange his ticket, which would be good on any railroad going in the same direction.

At bedtime, the passenger would become better acquainted with his roomette, a compact, private room. Already made up, the bed was hidden in the wall. It was lowered with a flick of the wrist, and the piped-in music was equally easily turned down, so that the passenger could fall asleep, or raise the window shade and somewhat superiorly watch the lights of automobiles racing across the Nevada desert.

Salt Lake City was achieved that morning. After a sightseeing tour of Salt Lake City, the passenger then might board the Rio Grande's *Royal Gorge* the next afternoon as the sun's last rays were painting the Wasatch Mountains. Just 745 miles across the backbone of the continent—the Rocky Mountains—lay the 'Queen City of the Plains,' Denver.

Like the *California Zephyr*, the *Royal Gorge* sported a Vista- Dome. This was particularly appropriate for it was in the Rocky Mountains that the idea of the modern observation dome was conceived on a July day in 1944, by CR Osborn, vice president of General Motors. Riding in the

***These pages:* The *California Zephyr*—advertising art, and a Feather River Route logo on a *Zephyr* diesel locomotive's nose.**

921-D
921-D
WESTERN
FEATHER RIVER ROUTE
PACIFIC

Rio Grande
5771
Rio Grand

Grande

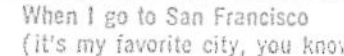

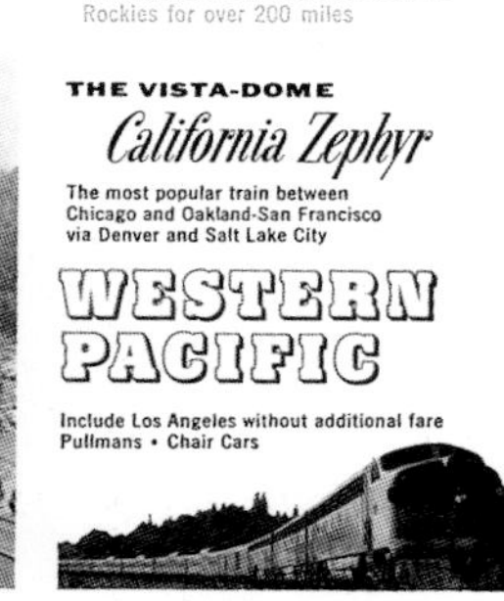

glass nose of a diesel, it struck him that a glass-topped passenger car would be popular. It was just a year later that the first Vista-Dome went into service on the Chicago, Burlington & Quincy, and today a monument still stands beside the tracks where Mr Osborn had his idea.

(Even so, the Canadian Pacific's nineteenth century express, the *Imperial Limited*, sported rooftop cupolas on at least two of its cars, though these were far removed from the extensive glass canopies of the late 1940s and 1950s.)

When the passenger went to sleep that night aboard the *Royal Gorge*, a pale moon was glimmering on the tumbling Colorado River, flowing west to Boulder Dam and the Gulf of California. When he awakened he was on the roof of the continent, Tennessee Pass, 3121 meters (10,240 feet) high, and sunrise was pinkening an eastbound river, the Arkansas, headed for the Mississippi. As the passenger breakfasted, breathless vistas unfolded at every turn of the track.

Far to the south, the snowy minarets of the Sangre de Cristo range were scarlet in the early light, just as Spanish explorers first saw them and named them Blood of Christ. Then, in midmorning, the train dipped into the feature of this route, for which the train is named—the mystic Royal Gorge.

The Vista-Dome was the place to enjoy it. The brightly colored canyon walls closed in, soaring until they seemed almost to meet half a mile straight up, and the floor of the gorge was bathed in eerie, rose-tinted shadow. Where the train stopped, a traveller could flip pebbles from one wall to the other. A fifth of a mile overhead, a dark thread against the sky marked an engineering marvel, the world's highest highway bridge.

East of the gorge, the train began to catch distant glimpses of Pikes Peak, the most famous of the Rocky Mountains

Previous page: **The Denver & Rio Grande *Zephyr*, from which extended the *Royal Gorge* special. *Opposite:* A partitioned master bedroom aboard the Western Pacific *California Zephyr*. *Above, both and at right:* Advertisements for the *California Zephyr*.**

Rio Grande
Grande

(although 27 are higher), and it was still visible when the *Royal Gorge* pulled into Denver.

At this point, the passenger would have a chance to ride a 'railroad cannonball'—ie, a super-fast train—the Union Pacific's *City of Denver*. The passenger would board that train the next afternoon, and might immediately have decided to go to the train's pub—a handsome, wood-paneled taproom on wheels—when the train took off.

In an automobile, the driver of the 1950s—not unlike the driver of the 1990s—would be satisfied to average 80 kph (50 mph) for a day's run. On the *City of Denver*, passengers rode 901 km (560 miles) in eight hours, for an average of 113 kph (70 mph)—a good speed even on today's interstates.

Scenery flashed past in a blur: the station agent's garden beside the Julesburg depot, where flowers bloomed between rows of corn; seas of ripening wheat; miles of beets and of factories converting them into sugar; the Rockies dwindling on the far horizon as the train whipped across the Great Plains, until at last they were only a violet haze lined in gold against the setting sun.

The *City of Denver* had the newest thing in observation cars—an Astra-Dome diner, the first in America and one of 35 new Astra-Domes then being added to Union Pacific streamliners. Also, the steward could *telephone the engineer* and keep passengers posted on their speed during dinner. With the chicken soup came the first bulletin: 122 kph (75.8 mph). With the salad, 125 kph (77.4 mph). With the grilled mountain trout, 127 kph (79.2 mph). Finally, with the strawberry shortcake, and for 153 km (95 miles) thereafter, the *City of Denver*'s speed never dropped below 129 kph (80 mph).

As the *City of Denver* headed on to Chicago, the passenger once again could choose to make connection with another train and railroad. Dropping off at Omaha that evening, before noon next day, he boarded another 'cannonball,' the Rock Island Lines' *Corn Belt Rocket*, for the 793-km (493 miles) dash to the Windy City in nine hours flat.

At left: **The Denver & Rio Grande *Zephyr*, en route as the *Royal Gorge* special. *Above:* A vintage postcard of the *Royal Gorge*. The train is as viewed from a crevice in the eponymous Royal Gorge.**

If anyone could, a conductor on the ultra-fast *Corn Belt Rocket* could teach passengers how to keep coffee from sloshing out of a cup: the trick was to put a spoon in the cup with the coffee. If that didn't work, two spoons would. This disturbed the harmonic waves that resulted in spilled coffee.

After a night in Chicago, the passenger could switch to one of the most famous of America's crack trains, the New York Central's *Twentieth Century Limited*, for the 1546-km (961 miles) sprint to New York City. The *Twentieth Century Limited* and its great rival, the Pennsylvania Railroad's *Broadway Limited*, ran between New York City and Chicago: the former, on its 'Water Level Route,' covering 1536 km (960 miles); and the latter, on a more mountainous route, covering 1440 km (900 miles)—yet both maintained a 16-hour schedule between the two cities.

In 1955, the *Twentieth Century Limited* sometimes had to run in several sections to handle the crowds, but on its first run, in 1902, it had only three Pullmans and 27 passengers. Even then, it had a barber-valet and a public stenographer, and it was one of the few trains to maintain those services into the 1950s. It also had private rooms with shower baths.

When the passenger found the barbershop, he plopped into the chair, and chatted with the tonsorialist, who might be coerced into revealing some of the famous heads he had trimmed. Such a barber, on the prestigious *Twentieth Century Limited*, would have worked on capitalists, politicians, gangsters and theatrical stars, charging them all the same—haircut US $1.25, shave US 85 cents. In return, the barber would be tipped one, two or even three US dollars, but the

Opposite: **A 1950 Union Pacific advertisement.** ***This page, all:*** **A theme club car and luxury lounges on a Union Pacific special.**

See the Best of the West...
via UNION PACIFIC
UNION PACIFIC
YELLOWSTONE National Park
PACIFIC NORTHWEST
SUN VALLEY
GRAND TETON National Park
DUDE RANCHES
DUDE RANCHES
TO CHICAGO
TO ST. LOUIS
Great Salt Lake
CALIFORNIA
COLORADO Mountain Parks
BRYCE CANYON Nat'l Park
ZION Nat'l Park
HOOVER DAM and Lake Mead
GRAND CANYON National Park
Take your choice of these famous National Parks and other colorful vacation regions. There's scenic grandeur to thrill you . . . and healthful recreation.
Go there in comfort. Enjoy complete relaxation from the minute you board your train until you arrive.
Union Pacific provides spacious, air conditioned Pullman and coach accommodations. Daily Streamliner service to Los Angeles, San Francisco, Portland and Denver from Chicago and St. Louis, praised by discriminating travelers.
For a free attractive booklet describing the region which interests you, mail coupon today!
Union Pacific Railroad
Room No. 150, Omaha 2, Nebraska
I am interested in a train trip to the following region.
Please send booklet.
(Name region)
Name
Street
City
State
UNION PACIFIC RAILROAD
Road of the Daily Streamliners

average passenger could escape the barber chair for a tip of perhaps US 50 cents.

The train secretary on the *Twentieth Century Limited* was both stenographer and telephone operator, and there was no charge for his services. Like the car phones of the 1980s, the telephone on the *Twentieth Century Limited* operated by radio to the nearest mobile exchange, then by wire and wireless to anywhere in the world, be it Teheran, Luxembourg, Mozambique or ships in mid-ocean.

The *Twentieth Century Limited*'s approach to New York City was down the broad Hudson River from Albany, past hamlets where great deeds were done in revolutionary times, making it one of America's most fascinating trips. Then, of course, few experiences could compare with the arrival at Grand Central Station, and the long procession past crowds gathered to watch this celebrated train pull in; the rotunda with sunlight slanting through its tall window; the grand staircase with its hurrying throngs; and the impatient hubbub of taxicabs shuttling in and out of the cavernous driveways like hornets from a hive.

For the first train of his return to the West Coast, the passenger might prefer the Baltimore & Ohio's streamlined *Capitol Limited*. Although the B&O was America's oldest commercial railroad, its tracks did not run into New York City, so the passenger merely stepped outside his hotel and into one of the big buses in which the railroad picked up passengers all around the city. They rolled comfortably through Times Square, Greenwich Village, along the docks under the very prows of moored ocean liners, and onto a B&O ferry, one of 1800 ships operated by the nation's railroads.

The ferry docked in New Jersey, and the bus delivered the passenger directly to his train car. Great American history was made along the route over which the passenger then rode in air-conditioned luxury. The *Capitol Limited* passed by Philadelphia, where Betsy Ross designed the Stars and Stripes and where the Liberty Bell is enshrined in

***Above, top:* Power for the Rock Island *Rockets*. *At right:* An ad for same. *Above:* A Union Pacific berth. *Opposite:* A UP diesel.**

UNION PACIFIC
951
951
UNION
PACIFIC

Independence Hall; Washington, DC, its stately buildings and monuments emblematic of one of the chief capitals of the Free World; and Harper's Ferry, where three states and two rivers meet in the Blue Ridge Mountains of West Virginia, and where John Brown's savage raid in 1859 cut the pattern for the War Between the States.

The B&O was also famous in the first half of the twentieth century for providing all-expenses-paid rail tours of Washington, DC, for high school and other civic groups, and a private car bearing such a privileged entourage was often picked up at the US capital by the *Capitol Limited*.

After dark that night, the *Capitol Limited* observation car, called a Strata-Dome, sprang a surprise—a powerful floodlight to illuminate the scenery, presenting vignettes of countryside in the path of light, until the light was paled by the glare of Pittsburgh's sprawling steel mills.

Few regions in the United States had better train service during rail travel's halcyon century than the stretch between Chicago and the Twin Cities of Minneapolis and St Paul, Minnesota. Streamliners once raced one another back and forth all around the clock. The passenger travelling this route had the option to select a train with a magnificent observation car—the Milwaukee Road's *Olympian Hiawatha*, which plied the route between Chicago and the Pacific Northwest.

The *Olympian Hiawatha* had an economy-priced sleeper named *Touralux*, a streamlined version of the old-time tourist car. Another innovation was a spacious rear-end, glass-domed observation section called a Skytop Lounge. The highlight of the train, however, was its observation car, called a Super-Dome, twice the size of most such cars, with

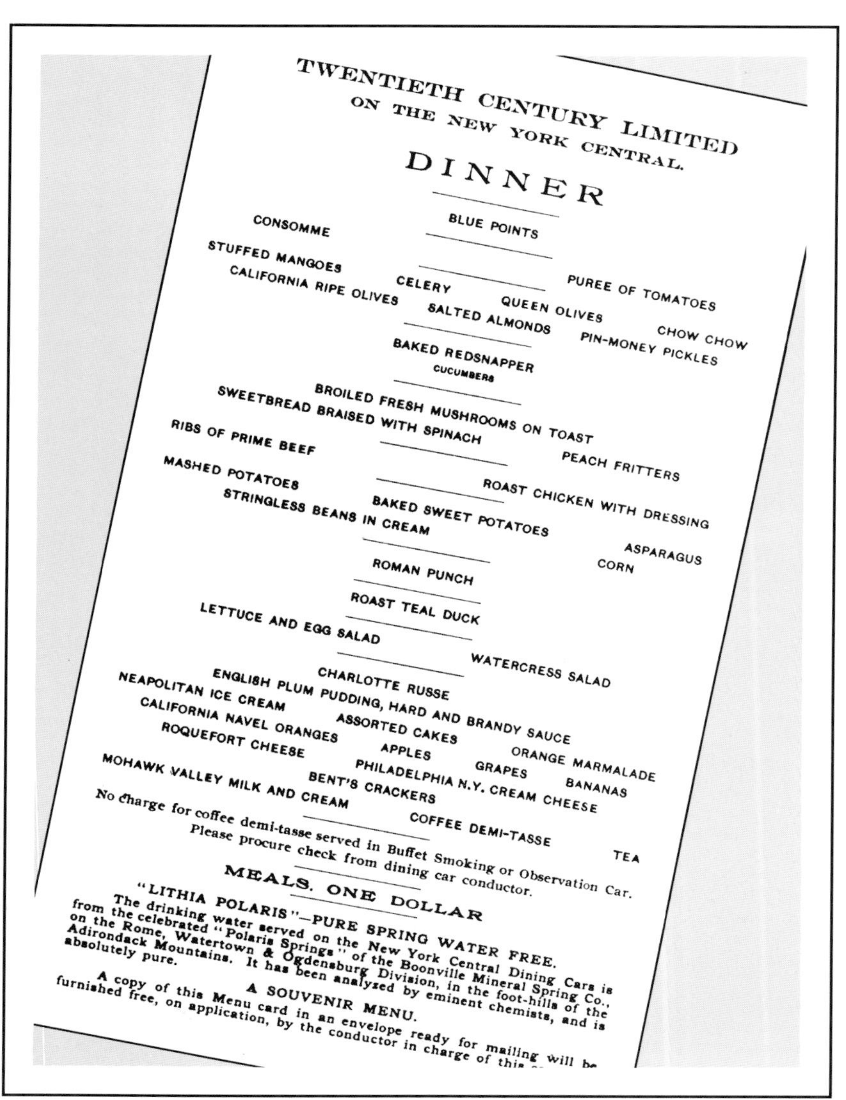

TWENTIETH CENTURY LIMITED
ON THE NEW YORK CENTRAL.

DINNER

BLUE POINTS

CONSOMME

PUREE OF TOMATOES

STUFFED MANGOES
CELERY
QUEEN OLIVES
CHOW CHOW
CALIFORNIA RIPE OLIVES
SALTED ALMONDS
PIN-MONEY PICKLES

BAKED REDSNAPPER
CUCUMBERS

BROILED FRESH MUSHROOMS ON TOAST
SWEETBREAD BRAISED WITH SPINACH
PEACH FRITTERS

RIBS OF PRIME BEEF

ROAST CHICKEN WITH DRESSING

MASHED POTATOES
BAKED SWEET POTATOES
STRINGLESS BEANS IN CREAM
ASPARAGUS
CORN

ROMAN PUNCH

ROAST TEAL DUCK

LETTUCE AND EGG SALAD
WATERCRESS SALAD

CHARLOTTE RUSSE
ENGLISH PLUM PUDDING, HARD AND BRANDY SAUCE
NEAPOLITAN ICE CREAM
ASSORTED CAKES
ORANGE MARMALADE
CALIFORNIA NAVEL ORANGES
APPLES
GRAPES
BANANAS
ROQUEFORT CHEESE
PHILADELPHIA N.Y. CREAM CHEESE
BENT'S CRACKERS
MOHAWK VALLEY MILK AND CREAM

COFFEE DEMI-TASSE
TEA

No charge for coffee demi-tasse served in Buffet Smoking or Observation Car.
Please procure check from dining car conductor.

MEALS, ONE DOLLAR

"LITHIA POLARIS"—PURE SPRING WATER FREE.
The drinking water served on the New York Central Dining Cars is from the celebrated "Polaris Springs" of the Boonville Mineral Spring Co., on the Rome, Watertown & Ogdensburg Division, in the foot-hills of the Adirondack Mountains. It has been analyzed by eminent chemists, and is absolutely pure.

A SOUVENIR MENU.
A copy of this Menu card in an envelope ready for mailing will be furnished free, on application, by the conductor in charge of this

Above: **The *Twentieth Century Limited*, pulling out of Grand Central Station.** ***At left:*** **A menu.** ***Opposite, both:*** **Historic views of this famous train's diner and saloon cars of the early 1900s.**

20TH
CENTURY
LIMITED

68 seats upstairs over an elegant lounge-cafe.

As the *Olympian Hiawatha* rolled past Milwaukee's lovely parks and on past lakes with such names as Pewaulkee, Nagawicka and Okauchee, the bartender in the Super-Dome lounge would regale interested passengers with the finest beverages—from liqueurs to fruit juice and soft drinks. Each window of the immense dome cost the Milwaukee US $400, and the two Super Dome cars employed by that railroad cost half a million US dollars. The train itself was one of several sisters, and cost US $1.5 million.

Such luxurious equipment accounted partially for the immense outlay on the part of American railroads of the period. In 1955, the United States railroads had US $33 billion capital investment, owned by 835,000 stockholders.

After a night and a day in the Twin Cities, and as the crisp northern twilight closed down, the passenger boarded his eighth train, the Northern Pacific Railway's deluxe *North Coast Limited*, for the longest continuous ride of this

***At left:* The *Twentieth Century Limited* rounds a curve on its famous 'Water Level Route.' *Above:* A historic advertisement.**

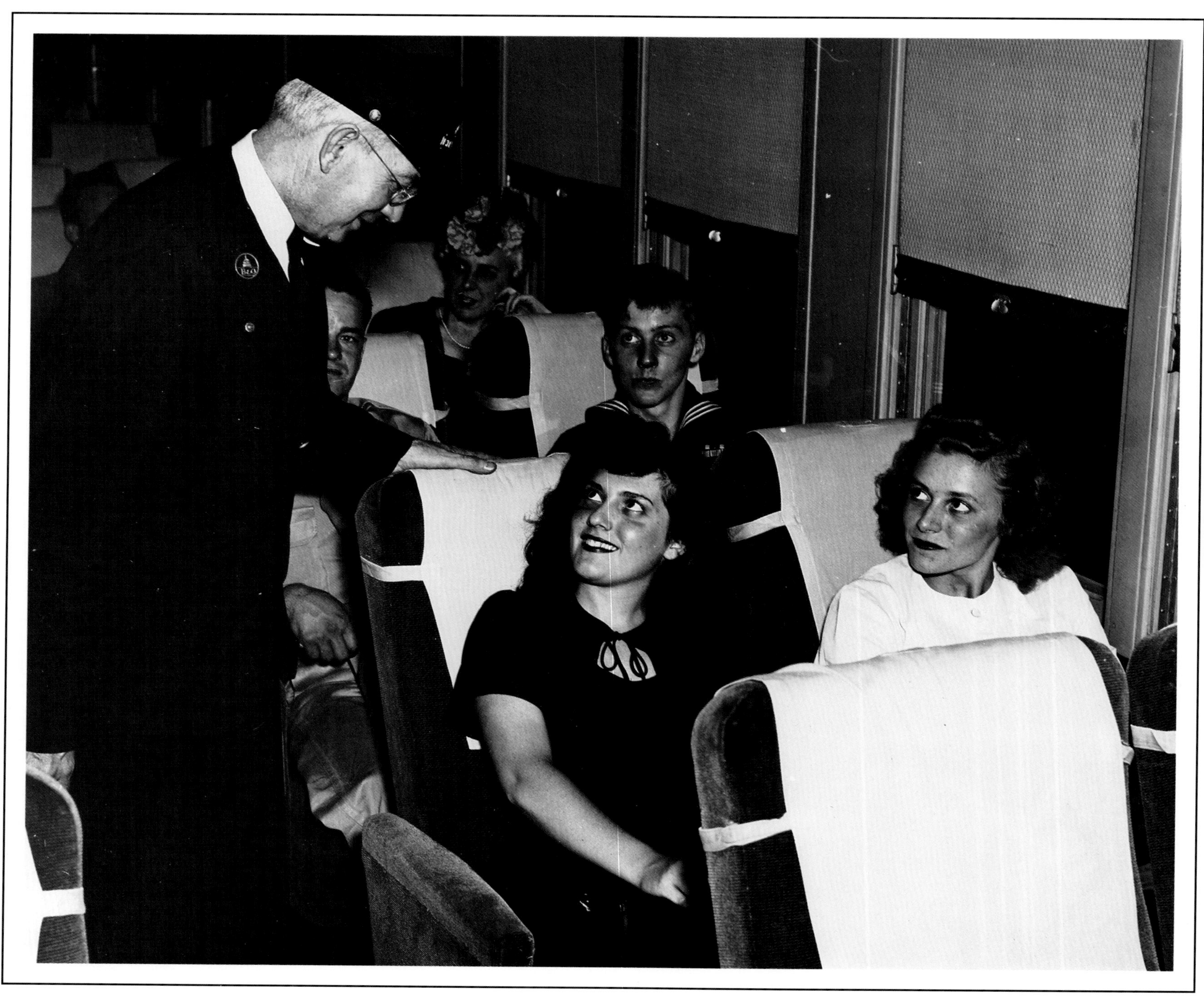

circuitous tour of the US. In fact, this leg of the journey would carry the passenger two-thirds of the width of the continent, through the central Northwest in a day and a half.

The *North Coast Limited* had something brand-new–a Vista-Dome sleeping car, the first of its kind ever built. It was, in fact and effect, a glorified upstairs sun deck for the occupants of 12 private rooms on the first floor—of whom, the passenger seeking the best of US rail experience would surely have been a member. Better than almost any other accommodation, this semi-private dome car conveyed the utter luxury of lounging under the glass, in air conditioned sunshine with one's morning coffee and newspaper, listening to soft music and watching the scenery unfold hour after hour—while somebody else did the driving.

By early spring 1956, there were four Vista-Domes on each *North Coast Limited*, two of them on sleepers, part of a US $7.5 million passenger improvement program even then in progress on the Northern Pacific. However, it would never be completed. By 1970, this luxury passenger service was gone and the Northern Pacific name was lost in a merger with the Burlington.

The passenger's ninth and final train was the Southern Pacific's sumptuous *Shasta Daylight*. Of this great train, we speak elsewhere in this text. Competition from the automobile and the airplane, plus outmoded fiscal planning,

B&O history—*at right and opposite:* Ellicott City Station, and the old station in Baltimore. *Above:* Inside the *Capitol Limited*.

B&O
B&O

caused the long demise of US railroad passenger service. In 1971, the federally-regulated National Railroad Passenger Corporation, popularly known as Amtrak, began its takeover of the nation's interurban passenger service.

Amtrak's services are not as opulent as those of the trains of the 1950s, and in some cases are quite Spartan. However, the service has kept the names of the great trains alive, and offers 'Superliner Service' on these routes. This service features 'Sightseer' lounge cars, which are high-level cars with large, panoramic windows and swivel seats in the upper level, and a lounge/bar for drinks and snacks in the lower level, where are also tables and chairs. Feature-length films and short subjects are presented as an entertainment bonus here.

The diner car has a kitchen on its lower level, and seats and tables on the upper level, for a unique dining experience. Day coaches have reclining seats. Sleeping accommodations are of four types: economy, family, special and deluxe. Each of these offers comfortable seating by day and highly adequate sleeping arrangements by night. Special and deluxe accommodations also have private bathroom facilities, and deluxe accommodation includes a private shower facility.

A four-channel sound system switch, located near the reading light, avails passengers of taped music and public address announcements. Additional amenities are available to each first-class passenger, including complimentary meals in the dining car.

The staff on these trains includes a sleeping room attendant, who prepares sleeping accommodations for day or night use, assists with luggage, is responsible for room service for drinks and snacks, and will provide a wake-up call, a morning paper and a wake-up beverage.

A typical breakfast menu for one of the Superliners presents the passenger with a choice of fruit juice or a cup of fresh fruit, and coffee, tea or milk. This is followed by a choice of hot or cold cereal, eggs, bacon, sausage, ham, pancakes and/or French toast with fruit topping, if desired.

Lunch presents a choice of fresh fruit or a brownie and coffee, tea or milk. This is followed by a choice of an omelet, a hamburger or cheeseburger with cole slaw, pickle and steak-fried potatoes; a grilled cheese sandwich with bacon strips or a slice of ham; a Sloppy Joe sandwich with milk and brownie or fruit cup and steak fried potatoes; a salad platter to the passenger's taste; and a pasta combination that is a chef's specialty.

The dinner menu offers a house salad with a variety of dressings; dinner breads with butter; and coffee, tea or milk. The main courses include the day's chicken selection; the seafood of the day; the chef's special—all with potatoes *du jour* or rice, and garden vegetables. Also offered is a meatless entree; a New York Strip Steak, done to taste, with mushrooms and baked potato; boneless prime rib of beef *au jus*, with baked potato and garden vegetables; a children's grilled chicken cutlet, lightly breaded, with potato, vegetable and milk or juice. Dessert offerings include apple pie with and without cheddar cheese, specialty pastries, cheesecake with and without a fruit sauce topping and a variety of fruit pies.

The Amtrak Superliners currently bear such great names from the past as the *City of New Orleans*, the *Silver Star*, the *Broadway Limited*, the *Lake Shore Limited*, the *California Zephyr*, the *Sunset Limited*, the *Pioneer* and the *Empire Builder*. Also, two trains that are meant to be representative, if not directly named after their famous forerunners, are the *Southwest Chief* (for the Santa Fe *Chief*) and the *Coast Starlight* (for the Southern Pacific *Daylight* trains).

A representative schedule is that run by the *California Zephyr*, which leaves Oakland at 11:50 and arrives in Chicago at 16:25 on the third day, going via Reno, Salt Lake City, Denver and Omaha.

Above right: **An *Olympian Hiawatha* promotional.** ***Opposite, both:*** **Pre-war views of *Olympian Hiawatha* lounge and diner cars.** ***At right:*** **Publicity for the *North Coast Limited*'s Vista Dome cars.**

Coming . . . a new service to Vacationland

Olympian Hiawathas CHICAGO – PACIFIC NORTHWEST

SUMMER will bring a new transcontinental Speedliner service. You can go, on faster schedules, to Yellowstone . . . western dude ranches . . . Spokane's lakes and Grand Coulee Dam . . . Mt. Rainier, Mt. Baker and other Puget Sound attractions centering around Seattle and Tacoma.

All equipment for the new OLYMPIAN HIAWATHAS, except the all-room sleeping cars, will be ready. This includes the roomy, angle-seating dining car and the distinctive Tip Top Grill . . . *Touralux* sleeping cars that bring new luxury with economy . . . famous Hiawatha Luxury Lounge coaches that are even further improved.

Free Vacation Information

For literature on vacations in the Northwest Wonderland via the OLYMPIAN HIAWATHAS, write F. N. Hicks, Passenger Traffic Manager, The Milwaukee Road, 722 Union Station, Chicago 6, Illinois.

Fascinating new club car for NP travelers!

The latest *Extra* on one of the world's *Extra Fine* trains

It's the most interesting railroad car you've ever seen—the new "Traveller's Rest" buffet-lounge on the Vista-Dome North Coast Limited!

In this striking setting designed by Raymond Loewy, you can read the colorful story of Lewis and Clark's Northwest journey right from the handsome murals, authentic maps and documents on the walls. You can relax in a lounge chair or soft sofa, or stop at the buffet any time of day for famous Northern Pacific food!

You'll find extra pleasure everywhere aboard the Vista-Dome North Coast Limited—for this is the train that has everything! Four Vista-Domes show you more of that spectacular Northwest scenery. A friendly Stewardess-Nurse makes you feel at home for a comfortable trip.

You enjoy all these extras at no extra cost. In fact, even low Family Fares apply on the . . .

Send now for "Northwest Adventure", free booklet of facts and pictures. Write G. W. Rodine, 859 Northern Pacific Railway, St. Paul 1, Minn.

VISTA-DOME
NORTH COAST LIMITED

NORTHERN PACIFIC RAILWAY

CHICAGO · TWIN CITIES · SPOKANE · PORTLAND · TACOMA · SEATTLE

NEW LISBON LA CROSSE WINONA RED WING ST. PAUL

The USA's American-European Express

Not long ago, an extraordinary event occurred with the inception of a new American luxury train. Many railroad buffs have felt some disappointment since the disappearance of such deluxe trains as the Pennsylvania Railroad's **Broadway Limited** and the Southern Pacific's **Coast Daylight**. Amtrak, their replacement, does not deal in luxury, although it can give one the feel of a comfortable overnight voyage by rail. Yet, now the United States has a luxury train once again, and it makes evening runs between Washington, DC and Chicago, Illinois.

In 1987, the owners of the **Nostalgie Istanbul Orient Express** joined forces with a Florida real estate magnate to create an American luxury train with Pullman cars and a European flavor. Extensive renovation of disused Pullman cars was undertaken, down to the installation of undercarriage equipment utilizing the latest technology—to assure a smooth, quiet ride. New heating, air conditioning, plumbing and other refinements were also made to the cars.

Luxuriant interiors with an Art Deco flair were commissioned. Rich,

dark mahogany, tastefully bordered and highlighted with brass and inlay work, was chosen as the base for these interiors. Brass lighting fixtures, marble surfaces and painted ceiling murals added further notes of refinement.

Fine period fabrics, echoing the tastes of the 1920s and 1930s—worsted wools, damask cottons and linens in exquisite shades of mauve, teal and brown—were selected for curtains, upholstery and wall coverings. Soft, embossed leathers were picked to cover the walls of the club cars. Rich and subtle carpeting was chosen for the floors. The Drexel Heritage firm designed tables, chairs and other period furniture for the diners and club cars. Original paintings were commissioned.

Each train consists of five cars—three sleeping cars, a dining car and a club car—designed for a mere 56 passengers. Unlike most other luxury trains, the *American-European Express* is attached to the rear of a regular Amtrak train that itself is named for one of the great luxury trains of bygone years, the Baltimore & Ohio's *Capitol Limited*. (In fact, the *American-European Express* cars are painted blue and gray, with gold stripes and lettering—a color scheme that evokes both the original blue and gray *Capitol Limited* cars and the renowned blue and white *Orient Express* trains.) There is no connecting passage between the Amtrak cars and the *American-European Express*.

The cars bear either American or European place names—hence, among the present company fleet, there are sleepers named *Washington*, *Paris*, *Vienna*, *Istanbul*, *Monte Carlo* and *Berlin*. The two diners currently on the company roster are named *Zurich* and *Chicago*; and the two club cars are *Bay Point* and *St Moritz*.

Each sleeping car has a shower, and all sleeping compartments are equipped with a private water closet and a sink. Mahogany, leather and fine fabrics, plus room lighting and reading lamps, highlight the sleeping quarters, which are of three levels, as follows. 'Car Bedrooms' sleep two in upper and lower beds that stow away for day use. 'Drawing Room' suites offer two full-size lower and one full-size upper bed, in a large room. The 'Presidential Cabin' has a drawing room, side-by-side beds and its own shower.

Ebony armchairs provide seating in the dining cars, which feature an executive dining room in addition to the beautiful regular dining section. Linen tablecloths, fine crystal, brass trim, mahogany paneling and European (oversized) silverware combine to create an atmosphere of warmth and impeccable taste. A full selection of European and American wines, port and cognac; and a seven course gourmet dinner menu (plus a la carte selections)—prepared by the *Chef de Cuisine* and his staff, in the full kitchen that occupies the rear of the dining car—add up to a high level of dining satisfaction.

In addition to sumptuous dinners, the dining car offers gourmet four-course breakfasts. On the other hand, the club car offers overstuffed chairs, a black granite bar, a Baldwin baby grand piano, and an excellent range of beverages proffered by a highly skilled mixologist. The walls, covered with embossed, soft green leather, glow softly in the radiance of Art Deco lighting. Also, a buffet kitchen and gift shop are located behind the bar.

There is onboard FAX and telephone service. The average fare for a journey on the *American-European Express* is less than air travel plus a night at a hotel and the cost of comparable meals. This service is a splendid alternative to ordinary travel accommodation in the Washington-Chicago corridor. Already, commuters with an eye for luxury and a taste for classic sleeping accommodations are lining up to join the fortunate clientele of the *American-European Express*.

Previous page: **A 'Car Bedroom' set up for day use.** ***At top right:*** **Inside an elegant *American-European Express* dining car.** ***At right:*** **A chef and a *sous* chef prepare a gourmet dinner in the train's full kitchen.** ***Above right, both:*** **A private dining room, and a club car (note the baby grand piano).** ***Opposite:*** **Memorable *American-European Express* exterior views.**

AMERICAN EUROPEAN EXPRESS
ISTANBUL

INDEX

Adelaide, Australia 6, 9, 16, 18
Alice Springs, Australia 16
American-European Express 52, 186-189, *187-189*
Amsterdam, Netherlands 39
Amtrak 184, 188
Amtrak Metroliner *149*
Amtrak Superliner *148, 150, 154-155*, 188
Amur, USSR 61, 64
Arlberg Orient Express 38
Astra-Dome *4-5*, 158, 165, 166, 170, 173, 178, 182
Athens, Greece 38, 39, 48
Atlantic 90, 92

Baghdad, Iraq 39, 40, 48
Baikal, Lake (USSR) 56, 57, 61, 63, 64
Baltimore Station 158, *160, 183*
Baltimore & Ohio Railroad 176, 178, 188
Banff, Alberta 93, *112*
Bay Point 188
Belgrade, Yugoslavia 39, 41, 48
Belogorsk, USSR 58, 63
Berlin, East Germany 39
Berlin 188
Bloutrein see Blue Train
Blue Train 2-3, 74-89, *75-89*
Blue Mountains (Australia) *16*
Boulogne, France 38, 51
Brantford, Ontario *106*
Bratsk, USSR 64
Broadway Limited 174, 184, 186
Brodsky, Josef 61
Broken Hill, Australia 16
Bucharest, Rumania 32, 34, 38
Budapest, Hungary 38, 41, 46, 51
Burlington Railroad 165

Calais, France 34, 38
Calgary, Alberta 93
Cairo, Egypt 40
California Express 126
California Zephyr 156, 165, *166-167, 170-171*, 184
Canadian Northern Railway 101
Canadian Pacific Railway 92, 93, *101, 104-105*
Cape Horn, South Africa 74
Cape Town, South Africa 74, 76, 86, *88-89*
Capitol Limited 176, 178, *182*, 188
Cascade 138
Central Pacific Railroad 122, 124
Chabarovsk, USSR 56
Chaleur 92, 92
Chara, USSR 64
Chekhov, Anton 60
Chicago, IL *5*, 138, 165, 174, 178, 184, 186
Chicago 188
Chicago, Burlington & Quincy Railroad 170
Chinese Eastern Railway 57
Chita, USSR 56
Christie, Agatha 38
Circum, USSR 56, 57, 61

City of Denver 164-165, 173
City of New Orleans 184
City of San Francisco 128, *130-131, 157, 164-165*
Coast Daylight 120, 122, 140, 148, 156, 184, 186
Coast Starlight 151, 152, *154-155*, 184
Cockburn, New South Wales 13
Cologne, West Germany 38
Commonwealth Railways' *Trans-Australian Express* 8, 9, 16, *16*
Constantinople 28, 32, 38, 39 *see also* Istanbul, Turkey
Cook, Australia 8
Coolidge, President Calvin 181
Coonamia, Australia 18
Corn Belt Rocket 173, 174

Dallas, TX 128
Danube River 41
Darling Mountain (Canada) 9
'Daynighter' cars *110-111*
Denver, CO 166, 184
Denver & Rio Grande *Zephyr 168-169, 172-173, 192*
Direct Orient Express 42
Dominion 80
Dostoevsky, Fyodor 61
Drakensburg 80
Dresden, East Germany 51
Durban, South Africa 74, 80
Durrell, Lawrence 52

East Perth Rail Terminal *18-19, 22-23*
Edirne, Turkey 48, 51
Edmonton, Alberta 93, 95, 106, 108, 114
Ellicott City Station *182*
Empire Builder 184

Fleche d'Oro 39, 51
Flying d'Or 39
Flying Scotsman 39
Fort William, Canada 93
Frankfurt, West Germany 38
Frau Munster 41
Fremantle, Australia 22
Fuji, Mount (Japan) *70*
Futsu 68

Gare de Lyon, Paris, France 38
Ghan, The 16
Glatt, Aby 46
Golden State 138
Gogol, Nikolai 60
Gorky, Maxim 60
Grand Central Station, New York, NY 176, *178*
Gross Munster 41

Haifa, Israel 40
Hakata, Japan 69
Harbin, Manchuria 57, 58
Harper's Ferry, WV *160*, 178
Haydarpasa, Turkey 39

Heidelburg, South Africa 74
Hiroshima, Japan 72
Hokkaido, Japan 70
Honshu, Japan 64, 70
Hornepayne, EM 101
Hornepayne, Canada 101, 103
Houston, TX 128, *145*

Il Settebello 66
Imperial Limited 94, 170
Indian Pacific Transcontinental Express 6-23, *7-23*
Innsbruck, Austria 48, 51
Interlaken, Switzerland 51
Iraqi Railways 40
Irkutsk, USSR 64
Istanbul, Turkey 28, 32, 38, 39, 41, 42, 46, 48, 51
Istanbul 188

Japan National Railways (JNR) 66, 69, 71, 72
Jasper, Canada 93, 95, 106, 108, 114
Johannesburg, South Africa 74, 76, 80, 86
Jungfrau Railways 51

Kai-soku 68
Kalgoorie, Australia 8, 9, 13, 18, 22
Kamloops, British Columbia 95, 106, 113
Kapikule, Bulgaria 51
Karimskoye, USSR 58, 63
Karlovy Vary, Czechoslovakia 38
Klamath Falls, OR 126, 140, 144
Komsomosk, USSR 64
Koolyanobbing, Australia 13
Kwinana, Australia 13
Kyuko 68, 72

Lake Shore Limited 184
Lausanne, Switzerland 38
Liège, Belgium 38
Lithgow, Australia *8*
London, England 38, 40, 51
London-Bucharest-Istanbul Orient Express 38
Los Angeles, CA 120, 126, 128, 138, 140, 150, 152
Louise, Lake (Canada) *102-103*
Lucin Cutoff viaduct *126-127*
LRC 90

Macedonia 41
Mann, Col William d'Alton 26-27
Mann's Railway Sleeping Carriage Company 26-27
Maple Leaf 101
Mayakovsky, Vladimir 60
Medicine Hat, Alberta 93, 94, *112, 114-115*
Melbourne, Australia 9, 13, 16
Melbourne Limited 8, *12-13*
Milan, Italy 38, 52
Milwaukee, WI 181
Minneapolis, MN 178
Monte Carlo 188

Montreal, Quebec 92, 94
Morioka, Japan 70
Moscow, USSR 54, *57*, 58, 63
Mountaineer 94
Munich, Germany 46
Murder on the Orient Express 38

Nagelmackers, George 24, 27, 56
Nagelmackers 24, 28
National Transcontinental Railway 94, 95
New Orleans, LA 126, 138, 158
New South Wales Railway 8
New Tokaido Line 69, 70, *72*
New York City, NY 160, 165, 174
Niš, Yugoslavia 38
Nord Express 38
Nord Railway *34*
North Coast Limited 156, 181, 182, *184*
Nostalgie Istanbul Orient Express 32, *36-37*, *41*, *44-45*, *49*, 51, *52*, 186
Novosibirsk, USSR 56
Nugata, Japan 70
Nullarbor Plain (Australia) 6, *8*, *9*, *18*

Oakland, CA 152, 165, 184
Ocean 90, 92
Olympian 132
Olympian Hiawatha 156, 178, 181, *184-185*
Ooldea, Australia 18
Oregon & Pacific Railroad 124
Oregon Express 124, 126
Oregonian 126
Orient Express 4, 24-53, *25-53*, 76, 188
Osaka, Japan 69, 72
Osborn, CR 170
Ostend, Belgium 38
Overland Limited 16, 126, *126-127*

Panama Limited 156
Paris, France 32, 34, 41, 51
Paris 188
Paris Exhibition of 1900 38
Pasternak, Boris 61
Peking, China 52
Peking Orient Express 52, 65
Perth, Australia 6, 8, 9, 13, 22
Philadelphia, PA 160
Pikes Peak (CO) 170
Pioneer 184
Port Arthur, China 57
Portland, OR 120, 126, 138, 152, *154*
Port Pirie, Australia 9
Postojna, Yugoslavia 38
Pretoria, South Africa 74, 76, 86
Prague, Czechoslovakia 39
Prospector, The 18
Pullman, George 24, 26
Pushkin, Alexander 61

Quebec City, Quebec 90, 92, 94

Ratushinskaya, Irina 61
Rawlinna, Australia 8
Rock Island *Rockets* 176, *176*
Rocky Mountaineer 113
Rocky Mountains (Canada) *92*, *158*
Royal Gorge 166, 170, *173*

St Anton Am Arleberg 51
St Moritz 188
St Paul, MN 158, 178
Sacramento, CA *124*, 152
Salem, OR *123*
Salonika, Greece 38
Salt Lake City, UT 166, 184
Salzburg, Austria 39, 40
San Diego, CA 122, 158
San Francisco, CA 120, 122, 126, 128, 138, 140, 148, 158, 160, *160-161*
San Francisco Express 126
San Joaquin Daylight 140
San Jose, CA 122, 126, 152
San Luis Obispo, CA 148, 153, *154-155*
Santa Barbara, CA 126, 150, 152
Santa Fe *Chief* 184
Santa Fe Railroad *130-131*
Saskatoon, Saskatchewan 95, 106
Scenic Dome *116*
Seattle, WA 120, 126, 152, 158
Shasta, Mount (CA) 144
Shasta Daylight 120, 126, 138, *139*, *140-141*, 182
Shasta Starlight 138
Shawnee 156
Shindai-Ressha 68, 72
Shinkansen 'Bullet trains' 66-73, *67-73*
Sierra Nevada Mountains (US) 122
Silver Star 184
Skeena 90, 106
Skoplje, Yugoslavia 38
Skovordino, USSR 55, 56, 57, 63
Smith, Donald 94
Sofia, Bulgaria 38, 41, 48, 51
Solzhenitsyn, Alexander 61
South African Railways 76, 80, 81
South Australian Museum 16
South Australian Railways' *East-West Express* 9
Southern Pacific *Daylight* 120-155, *121-155*, 184
Southwest Chief 184
Spanish Riding School 41
Spencer Gulf, Australia 8, 9
Spirit of Progress 9
Strasbourg, Austria 46
Sudbury, Ontario 39
Sud Express 39, 51
Sunbeam 128
Sunset Limited 138, 184
Super-Continental 90, 92, 101, 106
Sverdlovsk, USSR 68
Svilengrad, Bulgaria 38
Swiss Federal Railway 46
Sydney, Australia 6
Sydney Morning Herald 15

Tacoma, WA 126
Tarcoola, Australia 8
Taurus Express 39
Tayshet, USSR 64
Tehachapi 126
Tehran, Iran 39
TGV 66
Tokkyu 68, *69*
Tokugawa, Japan 71
Tokyo, Japan *67*, *68*, 69, 71, 72
Tokyo Central Station *73*
Tolstoi, Leo 60
Tomsk, USSR 56
Toronto, Ontario 95, 96
Toronto Express 94
Touralux 178
Train Bleu 51
Trans-Australian Express 8, 9, 16, *16*
Trans-Australian Railway 6, 8
Trans Canada Limited 94
Trans-Continental 9
Transiberian Special 52, 65
Trans-Natal see Drakensburg
Trans-Oranjè 86
Trans-Siberian Express 52, 54-65, *55-65*
Trans-Siberian Railway 52, 54, 56, 58
Trieste, Italy 38
Tripoli, Lebanon 39, 40
Turgenev, Ivan 60
Tuscon, AZ 138
Twentieth Century Limited 4-5, 156, 174, 176, *178-181*
Tynda, USSR 64

Ulan Bator, Mongolia 52
Ulan Ude, USSR 52
Union Limited see Blue Train
Union Pacific Railroad *1*, *130-131*, *174-175*, *177*
Urgal, USSR 64

Valley Daylight 120, 122
Valley Flyer 126
Vancouver, BC 92, 93, 106, 116
Vancouver, Hotel *117*, *118-119*
Venice, Italy 38, 51
Venice Simplon see Orient Express
Verona, Italy 51
VIA Rail *Canadian* 90-119, *91-119*
Victoria, Australia 8, 13
Victorian Railways 8
Victorian Railways' *Overland* 9
Vienna, Austria 32, 38, 41, 46, 51
Vienna 188
Villard, Henry 124
Vinkovci, Yugoslavia 38
Vista Dome *see* Astra-Dome
Vladivostok, USSR 54, 57, 58, 63, 64
Volga River (USSR) 63

Wagon-Lits Company 24, 27, 28, 39, 40, 46, 51, 56, 57, 61
Washington, DC 156, 186
Washington 188
Western Australian Government Railway's *Westland* 9
Windsor, Canada 90
Wolverine 156
Winnipeg, Manitoba 92-95, 105, 106, *107*

Yevtushenko, Yevgheni 60
Yokohama, Japan *70-71*, 71, 72

Zurich, Switzerland 41, 48, 51
Zurich, University of 41
Zurich 188

***Overleaf*: Out of the past: one of the great trains of the 'Golden Age' of American rail passenger travel, the Denver & Rio Grande *Zephyr* speeds toward Grand Junction, Colorado. Now, such trains as the *American-European Express*, the *Venice-Simplon* (and *Nostalgie Istanbul*) *Orient Express*, the *Canadian*, the *Blue Train*—and others of those we have herein explored—uphold an excellent global tradition of superb rail travel.**